Tunbridge Wells in 1909

The Year we became 'Royal'

Events and Attitudes in the Town
100 years ago

Chris Jones

Royal Tunbridge Wells Civic Society
Local History Monograph No. 9
2008

Published in Great Britain in November 2008 by
The Local History Group of
The Royal Tunbridge Wells Civic Society

ISBN No. 978-0-9560944-0-7

The text is set in Bookman Old Style 10 pt.

Front cover: The Pantiles, from a postcard posted on
2nd Sept 1909
Back cover: Belgrave Road, a typical view by Jim Richards,
photographer of 85 Camden Road

Printed and bound by the Ink Pot Lithographic Printers,
Southborough, Tunbridge Wells, Kent TN4 OLT

Contents

Tin of chocolates given to each child in Tunbridge
Wells for Empire Day, 1909. One of the first official
uses of the 'Royal' prefix - only six weeks after
permission to use it was granted.

Foreword

Tunbridge Wells is a great place to live. Nice houses, good schools, easy access to London and the countryside. There's just that one small problem. A question of image really. Doesn't everybody else think of us as being, well, just the teensiest bit precious? Of course it's not a fair description. Tunbridge Wells these days is no different from anywhere else. Perhaps we try to maintain standards a little more carefully than some others, and where's the harm in that? But then there's the name: Royal Tunbridge Wells. It doesn't really speak to a modern, egalitarian, meritocratic Britain, now does it? And yet it came about from those most modern of disciplines: marketing and PR. It was an attempt, cynical you might say, to protect and enhance the 'brand'. And it happened one hundred years ago, in 1909.

This book originally set out to explain the process by which the 'Royal' prefix was acquired. But it turned out to be a rather boring story - they filled in the forms, and, after a few quibbles, were granted permission. They weren't even that enthusiastic about getting it - there were no celebrations, no speeches, no processions, which was surprising in a town which enjoyed a good procession. In fact there were even grumbles that the King had not given them exactly what they had asked for (more of that later).

But if the main story was disappointing, the background information was fascinating. Investigating the 'Royal' proved to be a great excuse to research the daily lives of the residents, to see how they lived; but much more interesting, to try to understand what they thought. So the main section of the book represents a chronicle, month by month, of the events and news items that most seemed to interest the locals. The details are taken largely from local newspapers and official records, but a selection of national events is also provided. 1909 seems to have been especially news-rich: the introduction of Old Age Pensions, Bleriot's flight across the Channel, Lloyd George's budget, Dreadnoughts, and a constitutional crisis over the House of Lords. But maybe all years are as busy as that if one cares to look.

The last five chapters take a different perspective and look at the appearance of the town, ward by ward, highlighting what would have been new or of particular interest in 1909.

The book is restricted very much to the old Borough of Tunbridge Wells, so Southborough and High Brooms are excluded. Certain events in Tonbridge are included where they illustrate important local issues. Rusthall, I must admit, is largely ignored - I don't know it in 2008, and don't feel qualified to comment on it in 1909.

This is my book. All the errors of fact, judgement and style, are mine alone. But I could not have prepared it without the generous help of Philip Whitbourn, Brenda and Geoffrey Copus, Fred Scales, Gill Twells, John Cunningham, Ian Beavis and other members of the Local History Group. I must also thank the staff of the Reference Libraries in Tunbridge Wells and Margate, the Newspaper Library at Colindale, the Centre for Kentish Studies, and the National Archives at Kew. Keith Hetherington, Vera Coomber, Ruth Wakefield, Silvio Caflisch and Steve Niker have all been very kind. Special thanks of course to my wife, Charmian, whose life has been blighted by 1909 for the last twelve months.

As readers and writers of history we must be grateful to those who were responsible for the Freedom of Information Act. It was only by reason of this Act that we were able to see the Home Office files relating to the granting of the Royal prefix - they would otherwise have been closed until 2036.

I have included foot-notes where I felt a little extra background information would be of interest. However, to save paper, I have not cited sources. A full list of citations is available on the Civic Society web-site - thecivicsociety.org - and will be provided to the Local History Collection at Tunbridge Wells Library. I hope that the web-site will also be a repository for further research, and for correcting any errors. If you feel that a correction is required, then please feel free to contact us.

Royal Tunbridge Wells, September 2008

Christmas 1908

It is Saturday, December 26th 1908. The staff of the General Hospital in Grosvenor Road are trying to make the holiday period as pleasant as possible for their patients.

They have decorated the wards with paper umbrellas "in the Japanese fashion". On Christmas Day they had carols, a turkey dinner, and presents from the Kent Needlework Guild. In the evening there was a concert by the doctors and nurses and gifts of pipes, tobacco and cigarettes from Dr Murray Wilson, the House Surgeon.

Now, on the afternoon of Boxing Day, there is a concert by musicians from the Opera House. The Matron has invited Mr Wadham Elers, the Treasurer, and Mr Webb, the Honourary Secretary, to tea. Suddenly there is disruption and confusion - a group of Suffragettes has burst in. One of them has gained admission by complaining of a dislocated tongue. While she is being treated, others run into the wards waving flags, ringing bells, and shrieking 'Votes for Women'. One of them carries a whip.

Two policemen are summoned and on their appearance the leader of the party throws herself on the floor and has to be forcibly removed. The *Courier* reports: "The House Surgeon endeavoured to secure their retreat, but it is alleged that he weakly succumbed to the charms of a lady in spectacles, and at once protested his readiness to embrace - her cause."

Peace is eventually restored, but we have realised that this is but a charade - part of the entertainment laid on for the patients. The vivacious nurses of the establishment admit their complicity, and the Honourary Secretary appropriates a ringlet from the luxurious auburn tresses of one of the ladies. We realise that our Edwardian grand-parents and great-grand-parents had a sense of humour despite the stony expressions they display in photographs. Perhaps they are not so very different from us.

But some things are different. Christmas Day was a working day for many. Both local newspapers, the *Kent and Sussex Courier* and the *Tunbridge Wells Advertiser* were published on December 25th. Postmen had deliveries to make, though beforehand they were treated to sausage rolls and coffee courtesy of Dr and Mrs Claude Wilson of Church Road (and telegraph boys in Tonbridge were given bound copies of *Boys Own Paper* by a well-wisher).

3

There was a lavish Christmas meal at the Spa Hotel, with a boar's head carried ceremoniously to the table. After the meal there was a Fancy Dress Ball - over a hundred dancers enjoyed the music of Price's Bijou Orchestra. Festivities went on until well after midnight (which is why the ball was held on Christmas Day rather than the more customary Boxing Day - celebrations on Boxing Day evening would have stretched through until early on Sunday morning, which would not have been permitted). Norwegian peasants and Elizabethan courtiers were the most popular costumes, though Miss Madge Willats, daughter of the proprietor, was a Death's Head Moth; and the prizes went to Miss Rene Pizzey as Little Miss Muffett, and to Mr WJ Yapp as Othello.

Earlier in the week members of Emmanuel Church on Mount Ephraim had distributed Christmas dinners to the poor of the town. They had raised £68 at a concert in the Great Hall, and were able to provide 418 'dinners' - made up of a 2 lb loaf, a quart of flour, vegetables and an order for meat. Applicants for the meal had to be recommended by householders or other 'responsible persons'. However, over 600 applications had been received, and, with limited funds to work with, the organisers had had to impose geographical restrictions and exclude applications from people living in High Brooms.

Amongst the feasting and the festivities of Christmas there was considerable economic distress in the town.

An Introduction to Tunbridge Wells

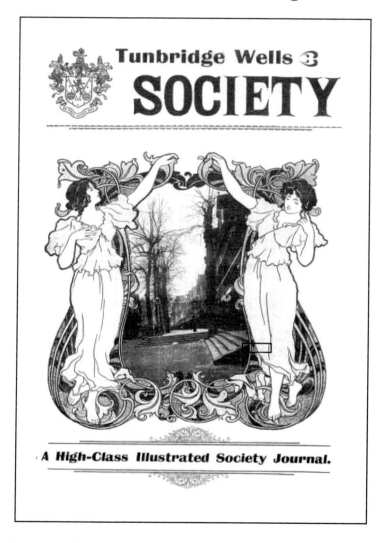

Front cover of the short-lived *Society* newspaper - Dec 1908 to Oct 1909
(c) British Library Board. All Rights Reserved EW 178

Tunbridge Wells is not a particularly old town. It developed in the 17th century as a resort for royalty and courtiers, who were escaping the formality and responsibilities of London; and it became notorious for their scandalous behaviour. It remained popular through the 18th century; aristocrats and intellectuals coming down to take the water, to gamble, dance and intrigue. But by 1800 it was losing out to the competition of seaside towns, and a more stable resident population developed. The coming of the railway in the 1840's led to a big increase in population with the development of both smart 'residential parks' and the more tightly-packed working-class areas around Camden Road, St Peter's and St John's.

The population of Tunbridge Wells in 1909 was 35,873**. In the public mind it has always been the home of retired Indian Army officers and maiden aunts. There is an element of truth in both of these stereotypes, though Tunbridge Wells may never have had the concentration of old India hands of, say, Cheltenham, Eastbourne or Bedford. The census figures for 1901 certainly confirm that there was a significant preponderance of women (three women to every two men - see Appendix A). Much of the imbalance was due to the number of female servants, but there is more to it than that, as shown by the following figures. They relate to a very small sample - the first 30 houses (25 of them occupied) on the east side of St James' Road, from the church down almost as far as Albion Road.

- Total number of females: 96
- Total number of males: 22

46 of the females were domestic servants. Excluding these (there were no male servants) the female : male ratio is still 50:22.

The houses in St James' Road typically have 4 or 5 bedrooms. Today they make very nice homes for families with children. In 1901 there were only 6 children. The 25 households were made up as follows:

- 11 were headed by spinsters, typically living with their sisters
- 6 were headed by widows, some with grown-up children
- 6 were families or young couples
- 2 were retired couples

All but two of the households had live-in servants. Three of the households had connections with India. All of the widows and spinsters were 'living on their own means'. Where the head of the household was an employed male, he was a solicitor, surveyor or in

** Medical Officer of Health estimate for the middle of the year.

6

a higher clerical position. Only one of the heads of household was born in Tunbridge Wells.

St James' Road was not typical of the whole of Tunbridge Wells, but it illustrates a particular section of the population - typically female, typically living on their own means (which were not necessarily great), and typically incomers to the town.

Twenty years earlier, in 1889, Tunbridge Wells had been granted the status of municipal borough. It was governed in 1909 by a mayor, 8 aldermen, and 24 councillors.

The Mayor was Cllr. Herbert Murkin Caley**, a prominent non-conformist, and Deacon of St John's Free Church (the building at the top of Grosvenor Road, now the United Reform Church). Caley was an architect; he designed, for example, many of the houses on the Boyne Park estate. He had not been first choice as Mayor - the Councillors had originally selected Cllr Marsh, but his wife had died and he had to withdraw. Caley took the role instead. He tended towards a liberal viewpoint - some of his actions and comments while Mayor were probably not to the liking of his more conservative colleagues.

The Mayor: Cllr Herbert M Caley

The town was split into four electoral wards, each with six councillors, two of whom had to stand for election each year. Both men and women could vote in municipal elections. Women had been allowed to stand as councillors since 1907, but there weren't any in Tunbridge Wells, though there were female Poor Law Guardians.

**The Mayor had a particularly fine moustache. An analysis of the 140 (all male) pictures in the 1908 Tunbridge Wells & District Who's Who shows:

    47% had moustaches
    29% had beards
      6% had mutton-chop whiskers
     18% were clean-shaven

Such exuberant hairiness was a feature of the older generation. Of 12 members of the much younger Kent County cricket team, 8 were clean-shaven.

Councillors did not stand on behalf of national political parties, though their personal preferences were usually well known. Rather they divided into two groups: Radicals and Progressives on the one hand, and supporters of the Ratepayers' League on the other. The Progressives looked to the Council to provide public services such as water, gas and electricity: the Ratepayers League was against all such activities which it called 'municipal trading'. The Progressives had been in the ascendant ten years earlier, when the Council had run one of the first municipal telephone companies. By 1909 though the Ratepayers' League was firmly in control.

Party politics were especially exciting in the later Edwardian period, and dominated the local papers, especially the *Courier*. If we are to understand what the people of Tunbridge Wells were thinking we need to understand those politics.

For twenty years up to 1906, the country had been ruled by the Conservative / Unionist coalition**. It was the era of Lord Salisbury, Queen Victoria's Diamond Jubilee, and the Boer War. By 1903 the government was losing focus. One of its senior members, Joseph Chamberlain, started campaigning for 'Tariff Reform', or 'Imperial Preference' - the imposition of import duties on foreign products - both to support British industries and to strengthen economic links with the colonies. This resurrected an old battle with the Liberals who supported the opposing 'Free Trade' policy.

It is difficult today to understand the passion engendered by the campaigns for Free Trade and Tariff Reform, but in the General Election of 1906, the Liberals, arguing that import duties would increase the price of food, won a landslide victory, taking 399 seats to the Conservatives' 156. For the only time in its history Tunbridge Wells, then part of the Tunbridge constituency, had a Liberal MP. In an exciting contest Alfred Paget Hedges won 7,170 votes for the Liberals against 5887 for Arthur Griffith-Boscawen and the Conservatives.

Paget Hedges lived in Leigh. He was Managing Director of Benson & Hedges - the tobacco manufacturers. He doesn't seem to have been an especially inspiring MP (though my main source is hardly

** Unionists were ex-members of the Liberal party who had joined with the Conservatives when Gladstone adopted a policy of Home Rule for Ireland. In 1909 the combined Conservative Unionist party tended to be known as the Unionists. In this book I have used the term Conservatives as being more easily understood in 2008.

Alfred Paget Hedges MP

unbiased - the *Courier* took every opportunity to criticise him). Within Leigh he was snubbed by the local gentry for being 'in trade'. He found it very difficult to justify his party's policies on Free Trade to the local hop-farmers who were suffering greatly from foreign competition. In November 1908, to make matters worse, the local Conservative party selected a new parliamentary candidate - a rather more flamboyant character.

Captain Herbert Spender-Clay was one of the wealthiest commoners in Britain. His family had been major shareholders in the Bass brewing company for many years. Spender-Clay served with the Life Guards in the South African War, but resigned from the army in 1902. His recreations were hunting, shooting and polo. He had a town house in Berkeley Square and a 2,000 acre estate at Ford Manor near Lingfield. In 1904 he married Pauline Astor, the daughter of Waldorf Astor, the exceedingly rich American who owned Hever Castle. They moved comfortably in the highest circles of society. (There is an intriguing link between Spender-Clay and the Marquess of Abergavenny. In 1897 Spender-Clay was persuaded by a fellow officer to sign some forms. The forms proved to be promissory notes which led to young Spender Clay being pursued in the courts for £10,000. He immediately brought in the police, and his 'friend' was sentenced to five years for fraud. The friend was Lord William Nevill, fourth son of the Marquess.)

Capt Herbert Spender-Clay

The Liberal government, which was led in 1909 by Herbert Asquith, had a radical agenda of social reform. The Cabinet had two high-profile young members: David Lloyd-George, Chancellor of the Exchequer and Winston Churchill, President of the Board of Trade.

9

Both were hated by Conservative supporters - Lloyd George for his radical politics and forthright speeches, and Churchill as a traitor to his class and party. He had been elected in 1900 as a Conservative, but switched to the Liberals in 1904 because he supported Free Trade. Lord Abergavenny tried to persuade his cousin Dorothy not to attend Churchill's wedding in 1908, describing him as "A man detested in society, a man with scarcely a friend ... Lord knows what a man to marry, I pity her."

1906 saw the first significant presence of the Labour Party in the House of Commons, with 29 MP's. This did not have any immediate relevance for Tunbridge Wells**.

** Though the emergent Labour Party did blight the career of one would-be politician from Tunbridge Wells. Edward Elvy Robb, Mayor in 1905, was defeated by a Labour Party candidate at Manchester East in 1910.

How we became Royal

Tunbridge Wells was still a significant resort in 1909, with a range of good hotels: the Spa, the Wellington, the Royal on Mount Ephraim, the Castle and the Calverley; plus dozens of boarding houses and apartments, catering for hundreds of visitors each week during the season.

What one thought of the visitors depended largely on one's own circumstances. In her *Memories of a Village Rectory*, Sheila Farrance described the world of 1909 as being divided into gentry and working class. There was a very real distinction between these two groups, but the social structure was much more complex than that. There were, for example, three quite distinct groups within the 'gentry'. There was the local aristocracy; there were the 'gentility', which would include those living on private means, retired people, and professionals such as doctors and lawyers; and there were those involved in trade, mainly shopkeepers. The traders, obviously, had the most to gain from visitors, from the increased business that they brought. But the need to attract visitors was an excuse used by all classes when arguing for extra facilities: golf links for example, or a better band, more watering of the roads even. For the same things that encouraged visitors - the Common, the summer entertainments, the pleasant surroundings - were what attracted the retired and wealthy who chose Tunbridge Wells as a permanent home, like the widows and spinsters in St James' Road.

The traders had their own lobbying organisation - the Tunbridge Wells Tradesmen's Association, formed in 1858. At a meeting of the Association in May 1908 the possibility of advertising the town was raised. There was a general feeling that it was not getting the number of visitors that it deserved. As individual traders most of them understood the importance of advertising, so why not advertise the town itself?

There was some opposition to this. One member thought that if the facilities within the town were improved, it would advertise itself. Strangely enough this was Mr Rust, hairdresser of the High Street, whose own adverts were very effective. He was supported by Mr Stone, who voiced the concern of many in the town, that "they must consider the class of visitors they wished to attract". At this point the meeting degenerated into irrelevancies, Mr Wickham (draper of Mount Pleasant) being worried about music on Sundays.

Albert Dennis

But the idea was taken up and the Tunbridge Wells Advertising Association was formed in July 1908**. Albert Dennis, a director of Waymarks (drapers of Calverley Road), was Chairman. Mr Rust was not on the committee, though Mr Stone and Mr Wickham were. It was perhaps Mr Stone's idea to send a letter to all residents, reassuring them that "The Association will take great care that nothing will be done which may introduce any undesirable element in the shape of holiday trippers."

The Association was active from the very start.

• It sponsored a chess competition, and was rewarded by a recommendation in the British Chess Magazine, that "Tunbridge Wells is an excellent place for a chess player to take his holiday."

• It ensured that Tunbridge Wells weather was reported in the London newspapers.

• It sent letters to 2,000 doctors explaining the health benefits to their patients of a visit to the town.

It also placed an advert in *Holiday Whitakers*. The details that it chose to provide - health statistics, rates, and local schools - makes it clear what type of visitors it was trying to attract.

In December 1908 a new local paper called *Society* was introduced. It described itself as 'A High Class Illustrated Society Journal - A Journal of Chat, Criticism and Comment'. It was produced in Eastbourne, and was pleasingly amateurish compared to the existing *Courier* and *Advertiser*. It survived until October 1909.

Society was a great believer in the glories of Tunbridge Wells "the most interesting, attractive, hygienic, peaceful place in all England". It was a strong supporter of the Advertising Association, and interviewed Albert Dennis for its first issue. Dennis had a great deal

** Advertising the town was not a new idea. In 1873 the Association for the Promotion of Tunbridge Wells was formed. It carried out extensive campaigns, producing an album of local views, for example, which it sent to hotels at home and abroad. It was this Association that organised the first Cricket Week.

to report. The Association had designed a leaflet, and was printing 10,000 copies; it was advertising in the *Daily Telegraph* and *Evening Standard*; and negotiating to share a stand with other southern resorts at the Imperial Exhibition at White City.

Society could not understand why the town did not attract more visitors, though it recognised that there were benefits in this: "Nature has bestowed her choicest of gifts and it may be that the blessed exclusion of the cheap tripper faction of the community, which has so often mired a popular watering place and started it on the downhill road, has conserved Tunbridge Wells essentially as a resort of the elite".

It may have been *Society* which first introduced the idea of a Royal connection. On December 26th it urged the Association to invite the King to Tunbridge Wells. His visits to Brighton in 1908 had been popular and had attracted additional visitors. The town had responded by renaming East Cliffe as 'King's Cliffe'. Adverts for Humber Cycles (see right) demonstrated that a royal connection could have commercial benefits.

Society was perhaps unaware of earlier unsuccessful attempts to manufacture a royal connection. In July 1897, at the time of the Diamond Jubilee, permission was sought to call the town's new theatre 'Her Majesty's Opera House'. It was refused on the grounds that there was no special connection with the Queen. The promoters immediately wrote back describing her "early years in residence at Chancellor House, Mount Ephraim", and stressing their loyal and patriotic motives. The officials were in a quandary - should they refer the request to Her Majesty, as they had clearly not known of her childhood visits, or simply adhere to their previous decision. They chose the latter option. A further letter asking whether use of 'Royal' or 'Victoria' or some other term might be permitted, was brushed off with the reply that nothing could be done until the Opera House had actually been built.

In February 1905, with the Opera House open for three years, and a new monarch in place, they tried again. This time the request was actually forwarded to the King, though with a recommendation to refuse, as there were no special reasons for acceptance. The King duly refused, his Private Secretary Sir Francis Knollys using the rather strange circumlocution "The King approves of this request not being granted".

So the precedents were not encouraging. It has to be said though, that a royal association was not essential for success. In 1893 the cigarette manufacturers WD & HO Wills had been refused permission to call a new brand 'Royal George', so they used the name 'Capstan' instead. Who is to say that 'Royal George' would have sold more cigarettes?

We don't know how the decision was made to try again. Albert Dennis was almost certainly involved. He had been part of the Opera House syndicate so knew the procedure. On 10th February 1909 the Mayor submitted a formal petition to the Home Secretary for permission to use the 'Royal' prefix for the town. The petition was not made public at the time, and no record of it has been found in the Borough Archives.

The 1909 request differed from that in 1897 in a number of ways:
• it was typed, whereas the letter in 1897 was hand-written,
• it didn't bother with claims about loyalty and patriotism. It went straight to the point - that steps were being taken to make the town better known, in order to attract visitors and residents, and that having the Royal 'title' would be of considerable benefit.

It specifically requested permission to use the term Royal Kentish Spa - not Royal Tunbridge Wells. Market research had discovered that many prospective visitors didn't know where Tunbridge Wells was. They tended to assume that it was in the West Country - near Bath and Wells (and therefore didn't appreciate one of its main selling points - that it was easy to get to from London).

The petitioners took one lesson from the 1897 failure - they presented their royal justification up-front. They managed to get both Henrietta Maria and Catherine of Braganza, wives of Charles I and Charles II, into the first sentence. They then went on to list the Duchess of Kent and Princess Victoria, King Charles the Martyr, the Queen's Grove and the Duchess of Argyle. They even mentioned the man who had led Princess Victoria's donkey, though admitting that he had recently died.

Despite all of this, the initial response of the officials was to reject the petition. The file note says "Tunbridge Wells seems to have no special claim to this exceptional privilege". If it were granted then other places of a similar kind might object. "Bath, for example, has a stronger claim." Fortunately there seems to have been some confusion - this particular official was considering the copy of the petition that had been forwarded by Paget Hedges, the MP. Consideration of the actual petition was being done by others, and was taking a little longer.

The Mayor's letter was received by the Home Office on 11th February. It took the officials ten days to consider their response.

The first official, presumably the most junior, said that in ordinary circumstances permission would not be granted - Bath and Wells would have just as good a claim. However he did wonder whether the King might have some wishes of his own.

The second pointed out that the baths at Ripon had been refused a Royal title, though the more important ones in Harrogate had been given permission (in 1897).

The third had definite views: "There is no reason why this town should be allowed the title Royal in preference to its rivals, and strong objection to associating the title Royal with such a word as Spa. It is extraordinary that one should wish to alter a good word like Wells to Spa."

Perhaps the King objected to this outburst (after all he was a famous royal frequenter of spas, spending each August at Marienbad). On 1st March, Knollys wrote to the Home Office that: "owing to the historical associations of Tunbridge Wells, to its antiquity, and to the fact that Queen Victoria visited the town in her youth, the King thinks that the Spa might be allowed to have the prefix of 'Royal'"

There was a condition though, that it was called the "Royal Tunbridge Wells Spa", and not the "Royal Kentish Spa". The latter conveyed nothing, and anyway, half of the town was in Sussex.

There is an intriguing comment in the letter - "The King thinks that the Ripon Baths can hardly be placed in the same category as the Tunbridge Wells Baths". It is true that Ripon Baths** do not compare

** opened in 1904 by Princess Henry of Battenberg - Edward's youngest sister. Currently (2008) threatened with conversion into flats.

with Harrogate or Bath or Cheltenham Baths. But what were they being compared with in Tunbridge Wells? The Spa Hotel? The Pump Room? Perhaps I am being too literal, but it does seem as though the King had something more in mind than the Chalybeate spring on the Pantiles.

One might ask what experience the King actually had of Tunbridge Wells. His last formal visit had been in 1881 - he arrived at the South Eastern station, went to Eridge Castle, visited the Agricultural Show, and was then taken back to the station. Perhaps he caught a glimpse of the Great Hall. Of course he could have visited incognito. His sister had lived in Rusthall for six years, but that was in the 1870's. He spent a weekend in Brighton in February 1909, supported by his new equerry - Col Streatfeild of Chiddingstone, who accompanied him on motor excursions in the area. Streatfeild was also in attendance when the King visited Berlin that same month, as was Sir Charles Hardinge of Penshurst - perhaps they talked about Tunbridge Wells.

The story didn't quite end there. The Home Secretary, Herbert Gladstone, felt that "Royal Tunbridge Wells Spa" was tautological, as 'wells' and 'spa' mean the same thing. A tactful letter was sent to Knollys on 18th March, and on 28th March, he replied that the King agreed with Gladstone, and approved of "The Royal Tunbridge Wells". (The King was on an extended visit to Biarritz, and didn't get back to England until 10th May.)

The Home Office wrote to the Mayor on 1st April. They telephoned on the 2nd too but he was out. There were a few things to be sorted out. He had, for example, to demonstrate that the Town Council supported the application - which is why a resolution was put to them on 7th April that a request be made. The Mayor was still hoping for permission to use the phrase "Royal Kentish Spa". He was advised by telephone and at a meeting on 8th April that this was not on offer. The formal notification of the grant was sent later that day.

April 8th was Maundy Thursday, so the letter would have been received on Good Friday. There was no immediate public announcement. The news appeared in the *Courier* on 16th April, in a single column article only 4inches long on page 7. Newspapers in those days were a little more restrained than they are today, but in 1908, the *Advertiser* brought out a Saturday supplement to record a notable murder in Sevenoaks**. Had the Royal prefix been of major

**Caroline Mary Luard was found shot in her summerhouse.

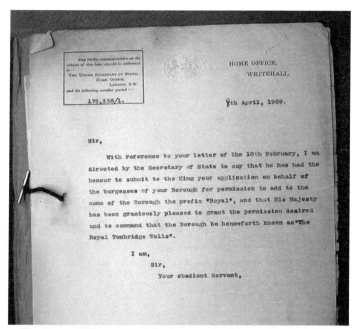

The Home Office copy of the letter to the Mayor. 8th April 1909
By permission of The National Archives

public concern, one might have expected the same thing to have been done. At least the *Courier* article started with an expresssion of pleasure at the news, though the paper dedicated twice that amount of space to a rather republican article about the need to find a suitable resting place for Cromwell's head - "the grandest head that ever sat on English shoulders". The *Advertiser* was less gracious, saying that the title was "a good deal more colourless and characterless than what I had hoped for", but "on the principle of half a loaf better than none, we must take what we can get".

The grant was not reported in the national papers until 20th April, when it appeared in the *Evening Standard, Morning Leader, Daily Express* and *Star*. The text in each of the articles is very similar, and looks like the prompting of some external agency, perhaps the Advertising Association itself. I can find no reference to the grant in the *Tonbridge Free Press.*

On 23rd April the *Advertiser* printed a rather antipathetic article entitled 'A Glimpse at the Future', in which a former resident returns to the town in 1912, and finds the shops and hotels have all adopted the Royal prefix, have put on airs, and either refuse to serve him or charge vastly increased prices. The Rangers football team, now calling themselves Royal Rangers have increased entrance money from 3d to 2/6.

Finally (23rd April) there is a letter in the *Courier* from someone (an ex-resident living in Croydon) who seems pleased at the news, though even here the commercial benefits behind it are acknowledged:

"many no doubt will be indifferent ... but why should we be ashamed of such an honour? We should rather be all the more proud of our town, with its many natural advantages ... Then let us put one more feather in our cap, and show forth the fine old John Bull spirit of knowing a good thing when we see it."

The town, then, seemed distinctly unimpressed by the news, which is a little surprising given its enthusiastic displays of loyalty at the time of George V's coronation in 1910, and the undoubted support for the monarchy of the majority of the population. Perhaps the commercialism of the whole enterprise was just too blatant. As we look at events, month by month, through the year we will see some of the problems caused by the specific form of words which was eventually chosen.

January

In which we consider:

- A Most Significant Date

- International News and the Problem of Foreigners

- Barn Dances, Bathchairs and Loganberries

- Unemployment

- A Young Woman's Sad Plight

January 1st 1909 was a most significant date, not just for Tunbridge Wells but in the 20th century history of the United Kingdom. On that day the first Old Age Pensions were paid.

The most you could receive, as a single person, was five shillings (seven shillings and six pence for a married couple). To qualify you had to be over 70, have an annual income of less than £21, not to have been in prison in the previous ten years, and not to have 'habitually failed to work according to [your] ability, opportunity and need'. Those receiving Poor Law relief, such as inmates of workhouses, were not eligible.

In Tunbridge Wells 286 were awarded the full amount, with a further 41 receiving smaller amounts down to one shilling a week. It had been an enormous exercise to review all the claims, and, like the experience of the Boer War, when the medical examination of army recruits had uncovered the poor health of a large proportion of the young male population, the OAP reviews revealed a shocking level of hitherto undisclosed poverty, especially in Ireland.

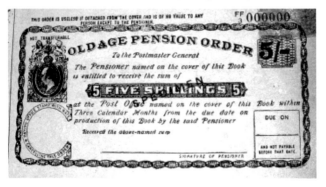

A 1909 Pension Cheque.
The cover of the book indicated the value of the pension:
Blue - 5s
Cream - 4s
Drab - 3s
Orange - 2s
Terracotta - 1s

The local press were obviously expecting some display of excitement on the first day, but they were disappointed. It was miserable and foggy, so many had sent relatives to collect their money. In its disappointment, the *Courier* did find one newsworthy incident. Mr Tickner of Dukes Road had collected his pension at 5pm, but died later that evening. "It is probable that the excitement of the day contributed to his sudden death" chortled the paper. Some of the newspapers did have a rather patronising attitude towards older people, so it is pleasing to note that the *Courier* was required to apologise the following week and report that Mr Tickner had been ill for some time. The *Illustrated London News* reported that it was "everywhere evident that the recipients belonged to a most respectable class". Just what did they expect?

The oldest pensioner in Tunbridge Wells was Mrs Collins, 92, of Norman Road. Born in Wadhurst she had spent her life in domestic service - in Mayfield, Tunbridge Wells and London. Interviewed by the *Advertiser* she explained how much things had improved over her lifetime, how much cheaper and easier it was, for example, to travel, post a letter, or buy a newspaper. Newspapers did not usually interview people like Mrs Collins, so it is worth noting her views.

The big international news at the start of January was a terrible earthquake in Sicily with 200,000 deaths**. Alongside statements of sympathy for the Italian people, the *Courier* reported concerns for Tunbridge Wells residents thought to be on holiday in the area. Gradually they were all accounted for, then news came that Rev CB Huleatt, one-time curate of St Mark's had been killed with his wife and family, crushed under the ruins of a house.

The local papers did not report on an assassination attempt on the French President on Christmas Day, nor on the public execution, by guillotine, of four murderers in Béthune. The *Illustrated London News*, though, described the scene: "Béthune was en fête, the executioner was the hero of the hour, and the crowd gathered round the scaffold with the zest and enthusiasm worthy of Mme Defarge". The *ILN* claimed that public killings were a barbaric spectacle reminiscent of the Middle Ages, yet it was only just over forty years since the last public hanging at Maidstone. The English had very definite views about their superiority over foreigners - views which were strengthened by the 'Tottenham Outrage' of January 1909.

Two armed robbers holding up a wages clerk attracted the attention of nearby policemen. In the ensuing chase, the robbers hijacked a corporation tram, a milk van and then a greengrocer's horse and cart. It sounds farcical but involved the death of one policeman and a 10 year old boy, and injuries to 21 others. The robbers were eventually cornered, and shot themselves. They were identified as Latvian immigrants, part of an influx of refugees from Eastern Europe that had taken place since the 1890's.

The case aroused huge public interest and antagonism towards the newcomers, who were labelled aliens and anarchists. The *Courier* quoted GL Courthope, the MP for Rye, and therefore for the southern edge of Tunbridge Wells, as saying: "Foreign countries are taking

**In comparison only 3,000 died in the San Francisco earthquake in 1906.

21

advantage of our hospitality and have got into the habit of sending their undesirables over here, filling the prisons with felons, and the workhouses with paupers. We have enough to keep without the scum and riff-raff of Europe."

I have no figures for the number of immigrants in Tunbridge Wells, though the 1901 census for St James' Park lists Mark and Jacob Goldberg, cabinet-makers, and Russian subjects; Mark's wife Jenet, and sister-in-law Hettie, both German; and his 2 day-old daughter 'not christened yet'. Neither scum nor riff-raff, surely.

On New Year's Eve, the Linden Park Cricket Club held its annual ball at the Town Hall. The dance card, printed in the *Advertiser* comprised: 11 Waltzes, 5 Lancers, a Veleta, a 2-Step and a Galop, plus two Barn Dances.

Over a thousand children enjoyed the annual 'Robins' Dinner' at the Corn Exchange on 5th January. Then in its eighteenth year, it had been started by Mr SE Haward, who had ironmongers shops in Goods Station Road and Mount Pleasant, and was intended for the children of the poor. The boys ate in the Corn Exchange and the girls in the Sussex Assembly Rooms. Both were subjected to an address from the Mayor. He offered encouragement to the boys, saying that there was no reason why they should not wear the mayoral chain of office - provided that they stuck to their lessons. As for the girls, he hoped that they would become beautiful women and take their place in the carrying out of life's duties.

There was also a meal at the Society of Friends for 200 cab-drivers and bath-chairmen of the town. They enjoyed beef and plum pudding, followed by cheese and celery. The 'bathchairmen' were the operators of the wheelchairs used by elderly and infirm visitors when taking the air on Mount Ephraim and London Road. Like cab-drivers, bus-conductors and station porters,

Bath chairs on Mount Ephraim

they needed a licence from the Council. They are usually described as very old men, but perhaps the open air kept them fit and vigorous. The 1901 census includes Mr William Skinner, bathchairman, aged 58, of Holmwood Road, and his wife Mary, 43, and their eight children aged between 4 months and 24 years.

It was also the season for Servants' Balls at the grander houses. 150 attended the Ball at Eridge Castle: indoor staff, outdoor workers on the estate, and guests from Bayham Abbey. The Marquis, aged 82, didn't dance, but was present at 10pm when the ball was opened by Lord and Lady Henry Nevill, and by Mrs Moses and Mr Smith, housekeeper and butler. Dancing went on until the early hours. At midnight a recherché supper was laid on in the billiard room, while the Baronial Hall, plentifully stocked with cigarettes, was available as a Lounge.

The first council meeting of the new year was on January 6th. The Sewage Outfalls sub-committee presented proposals to plant soft fruit on a quarter acre of the South Farm. This caused some amusement amongst the other councillors but with expected revenue of £25 against expenditure of only £5, the Council gave its approval for 200 loganberry plants and 100 blackberries. Letters to the *Courier* later in the month, though, questioned how much demand there would be for fruit 'grown on our own sewage farm'.

The Council then moved on to the possible lease of 9 Vale Road as a ladies' convenience. Cllr Bournes said it was too 'high class' for the common people. Cllr Carpenter explained that a well-appointed lavatory would be available for the charge of a penny, but Cllr Bournes wanted part of it to be free for the benefit of the working class. Cllr Bournes represented the North Ward and was backed by the Trades and Labour Council. It has been suggested** that the Ratepayers League chose not to stand against him in the 1907 election to provide a 'workers' voice' on the Council.

Tackling unemployment was not, technically, a Borough Council responsibility, but it was generally recognised as a problem. *Society,* in its typically exaggerated style wrote: "Unemployment is a disease that is poisoning the nation, it has got past being 'doctored up' ... other problems [the Navy and Ireland] are less important than the fact that thousands of British men and British women are dying of starvation".

**By Dr Ian Beavis of the Tunbridge Wells Museum.

Tunbridge Wells did not rely on large industrial enterprises, so was not subject to large-scale lay-offs in times of depression, but it was suffering from the national economic downturn. The general feeling was that building workers, attracted to the town by the building boom of the previous twenty years, were particularly affected.

The official response to unemployment distress was the application of the Poor Law, but this strenuously sought to avoid the payment of 'outdoor relief' and forced applicants to 'take the House', ie go into the Workhouse at Pembury. An alternative policy - the Mayor's Unemployment Fund - sought to support what was hoped were the temporarily unemployed, and to keep them within the community. The Fund was supported by appeals to the residents by the Mayor.

It paid for various schemes of work not covered by the council's existing workforce, for example:

- trenching work at the Sewage Farms
- painting the cabmen's shelter in London Road (see right)
- digging storm drains in Mount Sion Grove

The rates of pay were 5d an hour for unskilled work, and 6d, 7d, and 7½d an hour for painters, carpenters and bricklayers when performing these roles. Unfortunately funds were limited so the work had to be rationed.

Cabman's shelter in London Road

A group calling itself the 'Right to Work Committee', formed in October 1908 and based at 83 Camden Road, complained to the Council about the nature of the work, and the rates offered**. There were particular complaints about the work at the Sewage Farm being unhealthy, as the men did not have enough food, or appropriate footwear. WC Cripps, the Town Clerk, considered the criticism ungenerous and unjustified. He reported the current position of the Fund:

- a total of £573 had been collected
- 540 unemployed had registered, though 111 were single men,

**The rates seem to be consistent with those paid for building workers.

and therefore not eligible for work,

- 903 offers of work had been made. In addition, two to three hundred casuals had been employed during the heavy snow falls between Christmas and the New Year.

On 24th January the Right to Work Committee held a breakfast meeting at St John's Free Church. Roast beef and mutton, baked potatoes and bread and butter were served to 175 unemployed. The Revs J Kwell and W Potter addressed the meeting, as did Messrs. Bullen, Berwick and Heskett of the Committee. A Mr Taylor recited *"If Jesus came to London"* - probably the poem by E. Nesbit called *"In As Much As Ye Did It Not..."*. Nesbit, though better known for *"The Railway Children"*, was a Socialist, and the poem is quite strong stuff. It suggests that if Jesus came to London, he would challenge the wealthy people of the West End to explain why they had allowed their brothers to fall into poverty. It's a long poem and difficult to summarise, but the following selection might gave some indication of the feelings of those at the breakfast meeting:

> Then some of the rich would be sorry,
> And all would be very scared,
> And they'd say, "But we never knew, Lord!"
> And He'd say, "You never cared!"
>
> "I've got nothing new to tell you,
> You know what I always said -
> But you've built their bones into churches
> And stolen their wine and bread;"
>
> Brothers? They don't believe it,
> The lie on their lips is red.
> They'll never believe till He comes again,
> Or till we rise from the dead!

Then, carrying a black flag and with a police escort, they processed through the town, collecting from sympathisers. At the end of the day, the money was shared out - but it amounted to only 9d each.

Not everyone was sympathetic. One letter-writer to the *Courier* was especially incensed that the marchers had been allowed to enter private carriage drives to collect alms from individual houses. "This invasion of private grounds is a serious infringement of the amenities of living here, and is calculated to deter people desiring rest and quiet." If the police authorities had no power to prevent such behaviour, the writer felt, the Council should apply to the Home Office. If they did have the power, and yet allowed the march to go ahead, then it was a grave error of judgement. It is worth noting that the Mayor was a Deacon of the St John's Free Church.

The following Monday a large party of unemployed marched to the Pembury Workhouse to lay their views before the Board. The Board explained that they had no further work to give - they had reached the limit of what the Government permitted. There was a scuffle at the gates, but a large squad of police from Tonbridge was able to prevent an incursion. It is interesting to compare the measured reporting of the *Courier*, with the more excited prose of the *Tonbridge Free Press*, which describes an 'attempted raid' on the Workhouse, by 'a large army of unemployed'. Generally speaking the *Courier* was not inclined to blame the unemployed themselves for their plight, but to attack the Government for failing to act, especially Winston Churchill at the Board of Trade.

A further deputation to the Borough Council on Wednesday, fared no better. The leader, Mr HT Berwick**, acknowledging everything that the Mayor and others had done, nevertheless asked whether they could not do more under the 1905 legislation (the Unemployed Workmen Act), and levy a rate to pay for extra work. The Council could not agree.

Another initiative to support poorer people was the Boot Fund, which provided boots for poor children. The previous year, 1907/8, it had provided 351 pairs. The allocation of boots to the different schools gives a measure of the relative deprivation of the different parts of town - see the section on Eduction within September.

*   *   *

William Smith was house boy at Yaldham Manor, General Goldsworthy's residence near Wrotham. On Monday January 4th, he was cleaning the passage between the old kitchen and the scullery. It was very dark. He noticed a black parcel behind the footboard, and pulled it out. It was an old skirt wrapped around the body of a dead baby.

Clara Edith Bassett was the kitchenmaid. She was 23. When she started work at Yaldham Manor, in October 1908, she must have already been six months pregnant. She must have known that there was to be no happy ending. We cannot guess what was going through

** Henry T Berwick was church warden at St Matthews in High Brooms - described as 'the poorest parish in the neighbourhood'.

her mind: anger, regret, loneliness, fear of what was going to happen, the short-term need to find somewhere to live. She shared a bedroom with two other servants: the housemaid, Rose Penn, and the underhousemaid, Lizzie Ransley; though the beds were screened off from each other. They said that they were not aware of her condition. She was a very reserved girl.

The previous Friday she had said she was unwell, and had not come to meals. Cook had sent her to bed; though she worked as normal on Saturday and Sunday. On the Saturday morning she had got up early, and, explaining to the under-housemaid that she had had an accident in the night, had washed out her sheets - leaving them to dry in front of the kitchen fire. On the Monday morning, though, Mrs Keating, the wife of the coachman had called in Dr Walker to see her. General Goldsworthy was not at home.

Dr Walker examined Clara. She had prepared a story - that she had been 'indiscreet' back in October, and had perhaps had a miscarriage; but Dr Walker was sure that she had given birth. He would have to report it. She said that it was very unkind, that she would lose her 'character'. When they brought the baby to him, he could see that it was small and badly-nourished; but that it had been full-term, and had breathed. It had died from a constriction to its windpipe. There was a loose tape around its neck.

Clara was taken to the Infirmary at Yalding Workhouse. She did not attend the inquest. The jury found her to be the mother, and to have murdered the child, but wished to recommend her to mercy. The Coroner, Mr Buss of Tunbridge Wells, said that that did not concern them, but would be given full weight at the Assizes. Several ladies took an interest in the case.

The case came up at the Winter Assizes in Maidstone in February. Clara was indicted for the wilful murder of a newly-born female child. The prosecution told the story. But the judge said that he did not think that the jury would conclude wilful murder. Mr Gathorne Hardy** for the defence spoke to Clara who pleaded guilty to the charge of concealment of a birth. The Judge said that he believed that she did not commit wilful murder, but unfortunately did not

** I cannot identify exactly which Gathorne Hardy this was. Possibly the brother or nephew of the Earl of Cranbrook. He was probably engaged by the 'ladies taking an interest in the case'. Reporting in the local papers was generally sympathetic to Clara.

tell the truth in the first instance. How the tape got around the child's neck was not for him to speculate upon. He must punish her, however, not only to inflict punishment on her, but as a warning to others. He sentenced her to six months hard labour.

Unfortunately cases like this were not uncommon. An inquest at Crowborough in May heard the story of Hettie Oxley, 22. She had temporarily left some of her belongings with friends when taking up a new position. They included a stout box tied with cord. The friends noticed that the box seemed to attract flies. On opening it, they found what they thought was the skeleton of a small animal wrapped in a blanket. It turned out to be the mummified body of a baby. It had been born secretly a year earlier while Hettie had been working at a house in Warwick Park. She hadn't wanted to be parted from it.

Other News in January

"Boys Birched for Stealing Chocolate"

At Tonbridge Petty Sessions on 12th January, Bethel and Jack Hitchcock, and Harry Kemp, schoolboys, pleaded guilty to stealing chocolates worth 1s from a sweet shop at 2 Bank Street, Tonbridge. The boys elected to be dealt with 'summarily'. One was fined 10s, one given six strokes of the birch, and one four strokes of the birch. Such punishments would typically be carried out by a police officer immediately after the trial.

February

EDWARDVS VII - REX IMPERATOR

In which we consider:

- The Fear of Invasion

- Boy Scouts and Suffragettes

- Drunkenness

- Plans for a new Skating Rink

On 8th February the King left England for a state visit to Berlin. It was not a comfortable trip. Although the Kaiser was King Edward's nephew, there was suspicion and distrust between the two nations. Over the previous forty years Germany had grown to be the dominant economic and military power in continental Europe, and was now seeking a global presence.

The Boer War had been an uncomfortable experience for the British with the obvious failings of the British Army and the open hostility of continental Europeans. To some extent the new-found friendship with France (the 'entente cordiale') which had been encouraged by Edward's visit to Paris in 1903, relieved some of the tension. But Britain's friendship with France only exacerbated Germany's feeling of isolation, and Edward's visit to Berlin achieved little.

There was widespread fear of invasion, encouraged by books such as Erskine Childers' *Riddle of the Sands* (1903), in which a secret German invasion fleet is hidden in the shallow waters behind the Frisian Islands. Yet there was little initial enthusiasm for the new Territorial forces, created in 1908. Recruitment targets were set at 1% of the population - 398 in the case of Tunbridge Wells and Southborough. Three choices were available: the West Kent Yeomanry (cavalry), the Royal West Kent Regiment (infantry), and the newly-formed Kent Cyclist Battalion**.

By early February only the Cyclists were up to strength. In a speech to the Yeomanry, which had recruited only 60 out of 108 needed, the Town Clerk said that he was not at all proud of the town, seeing young fellows loafing about, smoking cigarettes, and sneering at the Territorials as they paraded. The *Courier* also attacked the manhood of the town, "who cannot spare the time from sport to take up the honourable profession of arms especially when the state was doing so much educationally for the young artisan". An alternative approach was proposed by the headmaster of Tonbridge School. He suggested that patriotic young ladies should reject offers of marriage from those who had not taken military training

But it was a West End play - "An Englishman's Home" - that had the biggest impact on recruitment. It told the story of Mr Brown of Myrtle Villa, who pooh-poohed the need for Volunteers, saying that

---

**There was also: the Sussex Yeomanry at Eridge, the Royal Engineers at Tonbridge, the Sussex Regiment at Crowborough, and The Buffs at Goudhurst.

no country would dare to invade - the British people would rise up against them. In the second act, forces of the 'Empress of the North' have invaded. Mr Brown grabs a rifle and fires at the advancing enemy, but is captured and, not being in uniform, is shot as a spy. The play had an immediate impact. The *New York Times* reported: "Every home in the length and breadth of the country has been stirred as not before ... The panic of fear that the country is in dire peril of invasion will not be allayed ... the rush to enlist continues unabated". The play came to Tunbridge Wells in April, but by then local Territorial forces were up to strength. Further recruitment campaigning was cancelled.

Looking back at 1909 from 2008, and knowing what was to happen only five years later, there is a danger that we over-emphasise the expectations of war. Certainly there were those who feared an invasion, but the fear was not universal and it didn't, on the whole, disrupt normal life. There was a rather nice, opportunistic advert from Noakes. It is headlined "An Englishman's Home", but it goes on: "should have British-made curtains at the windows, and British-made linoleum on the floor". The situation was comparable to the 1950's when there was a serious concern about nuclear attack - precautions were taken but most people had more important things to worry about - their jobs, families, curtains and linoleum.

There were those who actively campaigned against the militarist spirit. At a meeting of the Tunbridge Wells Peace Union in January, Mr I Hermann spoke of the friendly relationship between the English and Germans in generations gone by. A later meeting was more strident. Dr Evans Darby said that he would put on trial anyone who inspired his countrymen with hatred of other countries. His target was clearly the Boy Scout Movement.

The Boy Scouts are generally said to have started in 1908 with the publication of *Scouting for Boys*. Some troops, though, including the 1st Tonbridge, claim foundation dates in 1907. Initially they were all independent, but numbers grew so quickly - reaching 130,000 by April 1909 - that a national organisation was formed.

The problem with the Boy Scouts was that they were thought to be militaristic. Evans Darby quoted Baden-Powell: "Every boy ought to learn how to shoot and to obey orders, else he is no more good when war breaks out than an old woman, and merely gets killed like a squealing rabbit". The statement has been used by critics ever since.

Of course the movement was militaristic, it evolved out of B-P's experiences in South Africa; but it was also an exercise in social engineering - an attempt to attract the young urban male away from the evils of drinking, smoking and gambling. (Though there was a letter to *The Times* in September urging the Scouts to stick to the middle and lower-middle classes, and to leave the working-class boys to the 'brigades' - Boys Brigade, Church Lads' Brigade- who had more discipline and compulsory church parades.)

By March 1909 there were four troops in Tunbridge Wells. In January they held an exercise on Rusthall Common. The objective was to put a cordon around Rusthall village and prevent four dispatch runners from getting through to the Post Office. After the exercise there was a cross-country march and a camp meal. They were not allowed to use paper to start the fire - only bark and pith. Then they had some 'excellent drilling'.

Initially the Scouts were the subject of some scorn, especially when in uniform. An article in the Judd School Magazine explained: "The public hardly know how to take scouting - it is all so queer. Imagine actually going about in broad daylight in such outlandish costume. But every scout knows the comfort of wearing that same costume; so comfortable, aye, and so warm." The uniform included hat, belt, scarf (though not yet a woggle), shirt and knicker[bocker]s. The scout staff was very important, described as an ash pole tough enough to stand anything, it was often a broom-stick.

2nd Tunbridge Wells troop in 1908/9. The troop met in a room behind Head's fish-mongers (29 Camden Road). Scoutmaster Herbert Cable. Picture courtesy of Graham Edwards whose father is 3rd from right, front row.

In September, representatives from Tunbridge Wells attended a Scout rally at Crystal Palace. There were 11,000 there altogether, including one troop of girls "who excited considerable curiosity" (the Guides were not formed until 1910). The winners of the contest for smartest troop were presented with a field gun.

The Tunbridge Wells scouts went to Easter camp at Edenbridge. On Good Friday they were attacked by the Edenbridge scouts "resulting in a heavy fight, which will not be easily forgotten". Tonbridge scouts went to a camp near Teston where their skills were tested by members of the Legion of Frontiersmen. The Legion was a slightly shadowy organisation (which still exists) set up five years earlier to offer irregular military services to the Empire. By 1909 it had 3,500 members. It sought recruits from those with military service, or sea training, or 'life in wild countries or the Colonies'.

*   *   *

The King returned from Germany late on 13th February, tired and suffering from a bronchial cold. On 16th he opened the new session of Parliament. The occasion of the King's Speech was a focus of interest for suffragette / suffragist groups across the country.

The campaign to get equal voting rights for women went back many years, and towards the end of the 19th century had achieved a number of successes - women could vote for School Boards, Poor Law Guardians, and local authorities. But not for Parliament. Painstaking lobbying by members of the National Union of Women's Suffrage Societies (NUWSS) had persuaded a majority of MP's of the justice of their cause, but had not made it enough of a priority for those with real power. In 1903 the Pankhursts** set up the Women's Social and Political Union (WSPU) specifically to make it a priority. They started by interrupting political speeches, then moved on to breaking windows and assaulting policemen. Some of them were imprisoned. Their campaigning hardened attitudes amongst those who opposed women's suffrage, but brought the issue into the forefront of public debate. In June 1908 up to half a million people attended a WSPU meeting in Hyde Park.

There were two women's suffrage groups within Tunbridge Wells. The first belonged to the NUWSS, and was strictly non-militant. Its president was Madame Sarah Grand of Grove Hill Road (see the

** There are interesting references in biographies of Sylvia Pankhurst to her spending holidays in 1909 in a rented cottage near Leigh.

chapter on May 1909); its secretary was Edith Tattersall Dodd of Grosvenor Road (daughter-in-law of the artist). It held 'at-homes' at 'The Wilderness', the home in Pembury Road of Mrs Lydia le Lacheur (on the site of the present St James' Junior School). The second group belonged to the Women's Freedom League, which had split away from the WPSU in 1907 in response to the autocratic behaviour of the Pankhursts. It was militant and aligned with the Independent Labour Party. Its secretary in Tunbridge Wells was Dorothy le Lacheur, daughter of Mrs le Lacheur. So both groups were speaking from The Wilderness.

On 12th February two of the leaders of the WFL, Charlotte Despard and Countess Russell, addressed a meeting at the Great Hall. Mrs Despard spoke passionately: they were "not merely asking for the vote, they were demanding it, and demanding it as a right". The purpose of the meeting was to agree a resolution to be put to the government following the King's Speech. The WSPU had used the same strategy in previous years. They knew that the government would not accept it, it was simply a means of gaining publicity.

The following Wednesday a group met at the Dudley Institute and paraded through the town to the station. Six of them went up to London. Early the following morning they attended a meeting at Caxton Hall of 'danger duty delegates'. Their objective was not to be arrested, but to present their resolutions, but it was obvious how it would all end. They had all made arrangements for a few weeks absence from home. Miss Le Lacheur said that "It was horrible to think what these women were to go through. I felt more than ever how wonderfully brave they were."

The delegates attempted to form a procession along Victoria Street. The police immediately stepped in. Miss Le Lacheur, carrying the Tunbridge Wells banner, reported: "We were very anxious to do as we were told, but were surrounded by a crowd, and could move neither way. The police knew how these things were done and we were pushed back and back until we reached the pavement". When they arrived at Downing Street they found mounted police guarding the entrance. "Our leaders were arguing with the police but to no purpose. Then I suppose the women attempted to break through the line; anyway the crowd was pushed back. We couldn't see what happened ... one by one 22 women were arrested, cheered by the

** 'Suffragette' was coined by the press to describe the more active compaigners. Those in Tunbridge Wells called themselves 'suffragists'.

crowd. Among them was Miss Ibbotson**, from the Tunbridge Wells branch."

Miss Le Lacheur continued: "I wish you could have been there to see it: it would have made you ache to do something against a Government which could treat women in this way ... and there were men watching in the crowd, and from the windows, smiling as though we were making them a Roman holiday ... You would know that militant methods were more than justified."

Another local supporter, Irene Tillard***, 22, from Southborough, was arrested in August. She was part of a group which had picketed Downing Street, night and day, for six weeks. They were sentenced to seven days, but the case was rather complex and went to appeal. It is not clear what eventually happened.

The *Courier* always reported suffragette meetings in an open and positive way. Not so the *Advertiser*, which consistently displayed an anti-suffrage stance. In March it was particularly scathing when reporting Lady Constance Lytton's release from Holloway. Having been denied a pencil, she had written notes for a speech in her own blood. This impressed *The New York Times*, but not the *Advertiser*. This antagonism from a Liberal paper may have been a reaction to the suffragettes' deliberate policy of attacking Liberal politicians.

There were of course other opponents to votes for women in Tunbridge Wells. There were occasional anti-suffrage meetings, some heckling at open-air meetings, and criticism from the Primrose League of these 'wretched women who break the Prime Minister's windows', but no outright violence against them.

*   *   *

At a meeting in St Barnabas' in January the speaker described his work in defending the sacredness of holy matrimony. He believed

** Olive Ibbotson was 29 and from Rotherfield. She was sentenced to six weeks imprisonment. I have not been able to discover anything further about her, though she is listed in the 'Roll of Honour of Suffragette Prisoners' .

*** Miss Tillard, I think was the daughter of Col George Tillard, of Pennington Road, Southborough (earlier of Woodbury Park Road). She may have been the sister of Violet Tillard, who was arrested in October 1908 for a WFL attack on the grille of the House of Commons. Violet was a Quaker and worked for the anti-conscription movement during the war. She then went on a humanitarian mission to Russia after the Revolution, and died there of typhus. A very interesting woman.

that opposition to divorce was growing. There were still many people trapped in unhappy marriages. On 1st February the Borough Bench heard of one such case, as Evan Jenkin Lloyd 'graduate and tutor', was charged with threatening to murder his wife, Annie Ellen Lloyd.

They had married in 1895 and had four children. They had lived together until April 1907 and again, though without her consent, since April 1908. She was supporting them all by running the Calverley Employment Agency at 6 Calverley Parade (more or less where the Library is now).

It seems she had shown him a letter regarding a legacy. He was very angry. He said she had been his curse and ruin. "I could kill you. Nothing but God's power would stop me." He shook her violently, struck her on the head and kicked her. She tried to escape but he seized her again by the throat and struck her again many times. Eventually the police took him away. She gathered the children and took refuge next door. On her return she found he had burnt most of her personal belongings, blouses and underclothes.

Under cross-examination she denied failing to act as a wife in concealing his faults and denied ever hitting him, though she sometimes wished she could. Their servant, Mrs Emma King, confirmed her story. Their neighbour, Madame d'Aubigny, said she had never seen a woman so cruelly mauled and hurt by a man. Lloyd was found guilty and fined £5.

It seems likely from the story of Jenkin Lloyd that drink was part of their problem. This was not unusual in the Tunbridge Wells of 1909. Hardly a week went by without somebody appearing before the local bench for being drunk and incapable. On 8th February, for example, it was George and Sarah Steers of Cavies Cottages, St John's Road, who had been found by PS Neale, both of them lying on the pavement in Upper Grosvenor Road, 'helplessly drunk'.

Annual figures for the number of arrests for drunkenness were presented at the Brewster Sessions on 1st February. The figure for 1908 was 92 (71 males and 21 females**). Of those arrested, 35 were residents, and 57 non-residents. Unfortunately we can't tell whether these non-residents were visitors from afar, or locals from

** Temperance campaigners were particularly concerned babout drunkenness amongst women. One of them claimed that 'Britain was a by-word amongst other nations in possessing a drunken womenhood in its midst'.

the surrounding towns and villages. Arthur Cole of Speldhurst, for example, was fined 5s on 11th January for wilfully damaging a flowerpot in Mount Pleasant. The magistrates said that they were "determined to put down rowdyism on the part of young fellows in from the country". Yet the drunkenness statistics suggest that 'young fellows' from Speldhurst were not the main culprits:

Age	Arrests
16 - 21	1
21-30	11
30-40	20
40-50	30
50-60	20
>60	10

The Temperance Movement, typically associated with non-conformists, was strong in Tunbridge Wells. Its supporters had been disappointed in late 1908 when the Liberal government's Licensing Bill had been rejected by the House of Lords. So at the Brewster Sessions, it used a 1904 (ie Conservative) Act when presenting a memorandum to the magistrates.

The 1904 Act had sought to reduce the number of licensed premises, and had introduced compensation for premises that were forced to close. A ratio of one licensed premises to 750 residents was considered ideal. In Tunbridge Wells the ratio was one premises to every 406 residents (ie nearly twice the recommended number of licensed premises). The Temperance group claimed that the magistrates were not taking seriously the need to reduce the numbers. The previous year they had received licence applications from the Newcastle Tavern, the Foresters Arms, the Anchor and the Crystal Palace, the last three being adjacent (65, 67 and 69 Camden Road). Yet all they had done was refuse the licence of the Newcastle Tavern (76 High Street), which everyone knew was suffering such poor trade that it could not pay its rates. How convenient that Kelseys should receive £250 compensation to close it. The Temperance movement may have been strong in Tunbridge Wells, but it was not pre-eminent (the *Courier* was not a supporter)- the magistrates refused to accept their memorandum.

The magistrates did not, though, grant licences willy-nilly. In March the newly refurbished Bedford Hotel in the High Street sought a full licence (ie the right to sell spirits as well as beer and wine). They had to demonstrate that there was an unsatisfied customer demand in the area. Although they could reasonably say that they served passengers from the 'up' platform of the South Eastern station, and received '40 or 50 requests a day for whisky', they couldn't explain why these customers couldn't cross the road to the Bell Hotel (or six others within 350 yds). The application was refused.

Other News in February

'Old Folks' Annual Dinner

The Tunbridge Wells Tradesmen's Association held its annual dinner for 400 old people on 3rd February. This was reported by the *Courier* in its patronising way: "they gathered in the two halls, a happy family party, wrinkled faces lit up with smiles". The meal started with an entrée of stewed rabbit and pork which was apparently the most enjoyable course, being particularly suited to toothless gums.

A New Roller Skating Rink

Mr Welton Dale**, the dynamic manager of the Opera House, announced that work had started on a temporary building behind the Great Hall, to be used as a skating rink. Roller-skating was particularly popular in 1909. There had previously been a rink in Grove Hill Road but it was no longer used. The walls of the new building were to be removable, allowing it to be used for an orchestra and tea-room in the summer. The *Courier* was full of praise for the enterprise.

** 'Welton Dale' was the stage name of John Egginton. He claimed it referred to his family background in Yorkshire. In August he announced that he wished to be known by his real name, though with his Territorial Army title of Captain. In later years he went on to develop the Culverden Park estate.

March

ROYAL TUNBRIDGE WELLS IN WINTER - POST OFFICE & LONDON ROAD.

London Road: Post Office, Heath Villa and Sydenham Villa

In which we consider:

- **Wintry Weather**

- **A Train Crash in Tonbridge**

- **Competition for Shoppers**

- **The Spread of the Motor Car**

- **The new Skating Rink Refused**

The weather turned very cold at the beginning of March, with heavy snowfalls on Wednesday 3rd. The following day it was 12 to 14 inches deep. There had been snow in the period between Christmas and New Year, but this new fall was the worst for ten years. Traffic was seriously affected until a snow-plough pulled by four horses had done its work. Even then buses to Southborough were suspended, and the mail could not be delivered. It was a triumph for the motor-car - while horses tugged laboriously at their loads, cart wheels clogged with snow, motor cars 'ran merrily along'. Traders used sledges for deliveries instead of their usual hand-carts.

Tobogganning was popular - on the steep slopes of the Common between Mount Ephraim and London Road in particular. The police laid sand at the bottom of the slope to stop them sliding onto the road. They also took the opportunity to arrest people for 'driving a sleigh on a footpath'. Three cases came before the magistrates the following Monday. All three cases were dismissed, though a Mr Albert Chandler was reprimanded by the Bench for being insolent to a police officer.

The weather meant extra work for casual labourers - 400 were employed in clearing snow on the Thursday, but it also brought hardship to many. Tonbridge Council extended its soup kitchen, which was providing 1,000 meals a day, for an extra fortnight. At the same time, however, it chose not to take up the option under the Education Act of 1906 of providing breakfast for poor children, saying that this removed responsibility from their parents. Tunbridge Wells adopted the same policy, though Cllr Bournes said he was quite sure that some children went to school unfed.

Bad weather had a generally negative effect on health. The statistics provided by the Medical Officer of Health showed that death rates in the winter months were almost double those in the summer (162 in the first quarter, 93 in the third). This was typically due to disease, but there was a more immediate impact on the health of Mr George Keeling - a cast-iron gutter in Rock Villa Road fell on his head and fractured his skull.

* * *

The options for travelling to London by train in 1909 were many and varied. You could take a train from the 'Brighton' station (see page 146) up to Victoria, with the option of changing at Clapham for London Bridge. Or you could go from the 'South Eastern' station, and travel via Tonbridge and Redhill, or via Tonbridge and Sevenoaks; to either Charing Cross, or Cannon Street, or London Bridge. Or, you could take an express from the South Eastern station to Victoria via Penge. With trains criss-crossing the tracks between Tunbridge Wells and London like this it is surprising that they didn't hit each other. On March 5th 1909 they did.

The 8:30 fast train for Dover, via Croydon and Redhill, was a little late when it left Charing Cross that morning with Driver Moore and Fireman Howard on the footplate. They were due to reach Tonbridge at 09:55, but it was nearly 10 before they passed Penshurst. They were warned of a possible blockage ahead so they slowed to between 5 and 8 miles an hour. Driver Moore's vision was obscured by steam from the brakes, and he couldn't really see the signal controlling the junction with the main line from Sevenoaks. He thought that it was 'down' (ie indicating that the way was clear). Fifty yards from the junction he noticed that the signals controlling the 'up' line, ie the line to London which crossed their path, were also 'down' clearing the way for the express from Margate to come through. He was too close to the junction to stop, so put on steam to clear it before the Margate train arrived.

He didn't see the train that hit him. It wasn't the Margate express. It was the 9:05 Continental Mail train from Cannon Street to Dover, via Chislehurst and Sevenoaks, approaching on his left-hand side. It had been due at 9:50 but was also a little late. It hit the tender of the Redhill train, separating the engine from the rest of the train and leaving derailed carriages lying across the tracks.

At first they thought that no-one had been hurt. Then someone saw blood trickling onto the snow from under the wreckage, and two bodies were discovered - Fireman Howard and Inspector Rowley, who had also been in the cab. There were no other injuries. A quick-thinking signalman had stopped the Margate train just before it reached the station. 1579 telegrams were sent from Tonbridge station that day, by passengers advising friends and family that they were safe. The press preferred to use the telephone to get their stories through. The reason it was such a big story, was that a Royal train was due throughTonbridge at 10:25 with the King on board - en-route for Paris and Biarritz. It was re-routed at Bickley.

The railways were a dangerous working environment. In 1907, 422 railwaymen were killed, and 5560 injured. Comparable figures for 2007 were 2 killed and 1431 injured. Of course the numbers were greater in 1907, c400,000 compared with c130,000 in 2007.

The railway affected people's lives in many ways. A significant proportion of the income of the Tunbridge Wells Rangers football team, for example, was spent on fares to away matches. Coffins were routinely carried by train, so a funeral announcement might state that a funeral would start at the South Eastern station on the arrival of the 2:05 train (the 24-hour clock was not used in 1909).

The service provided by the local railway companies was frequently criticised. In the House of Lords in March, the Earl of Donoughmore complained about the (lack of) speed of the trains on the SER and LB&SCR, their (lack of) comfort, and their (lack of) catering. The debate was about a proposed merger between the two companies. Such proposals were opposed by Tunbridge Wells traders who hoped that competition between them would keep down freight rates.

The traders also opposed certain excursion fares. In January the *Courier* carried a big advert for a 'special, fast and comfortable train, to London's Greatest Shopping Event', ie Harrods Sale. The train left Tunbridge Wells at 10:43, arriving back at a quarter past midnight. The *Courier* described the Harrods Emporium as the largest in Great Britain, comprising eighty great shops under one roof.

The response from the Tunbridge Wells traders was immediate. In a letter that same week, Mr Charles Haines of JW Goldsmith pointed out that the railway company was also a customer of the tradespeople of Tunbridge Wells, who might object to this 'unfair method of drawing our customers away' and might get together to introduce a motor-road service. Another letter the following week from 'An Aggrieved Tradesman' pointed out that when people shopped in London they had to pay cash, whereas they expected quarterly accounts in

Tunbridge Wells. He was personally owed some hundreds of pounds. "Is it right or honest" he asked.

In practice the excursion train was less of a threat than the traders feared. Only nine tickets were sold in Tunbridge Wells, and five of those were to men - who were assumed not to be interested in shopping. The general conclusion in the local papers was that London could not offer the same quality of shopping experience as Tunbridge Wells. The *Courier* explained: "In London, in the majority of cases, ladies are served all alike, no matter what their position at home may be, or whether they are refined or otherwise." And in *Society*: "In Tunbridge Wells her presence in the shop is looked upon as an honour by the proprietors. Assistants in every department are at her command, and no trouble is thought too great to gratify her every wish. In London she is a nonentity, an atom of humanity, a wiggling worm."

On March 15th a new threat arose - Selfridge's, which introduced a radically different shopping experience to Britain. The sales floors were airy and spacious - there were flowers and foliage, and orchestras, a restaurant and roof garden. Gordon Selfridge backed his new store with copious advertising. Over half a million invitations were issued for the gala

Selfridge's - a rival to shops in Tunbridge Wells

opening. Daily adverts appeared in *The Times*. One interesting point was his boast "no gratuities expected or allowed".**

The weather on March 15th was wretched, but Selfridge's was packed. Existing retailers did their best to compete: DH Evans announced the opening of its Annual Spring Exhibition; and Warings opened a big extension, offering "The Most Unique Exhibition of Practical &Artistic Furnishing in the World". It was left to a shop in Camden Road to respond on behalf of Tunbridge Wells. Edmund Allen's was

** Other traders complained that the 'Selfridges' post-mark applied by the post-office within the store was also a form of advertising.

a draper and china shop at the corner of Camden and Garden Roads. They asked what benefit the shopper got from the higher prices in London. The goods were exactly the same; and they were available in Camden Road at exactly the same time as in London. The advert used Britannia and the lion to appeal to the patriotic Tunbridge Wells shopper (Selfridge was an American)**.

There is a mystery about Edmund Allen. This range of shops in Camden Road had been known as 'Tester's' since 1881 and was to continue under that name until 1948. For two years - 1908 and 1909 - it was run by Mr Edmund Allen, described by *Society* as having 'youth and brains'. But where he came from, and where he then went to, is not clear. (See also page 103.)

Since the abolition of the Red Flag Act in 1896, the spread of motor-cars had been rapid. Between 1905 and 1908 the numbers had doubled, from 74,000 to over 150,000. Kent had 4,071. It was suggested that if you wanted a low registration number "less disfiguring to your car" you might go to one of the Irish counties, which had fewer than 300. In Tunbridge Wells, Clarke and Rawson in London Road sold Siddeleys, while Rock, Thorpe and Chatfield at the top of Grosvenor Road would take an Austin chassis and build the bodywork to order. Powell's Garage in Grove Hill Road sold Rovers, and would teach new owners to drive.

** Further American competition arrived in Britain in November when the first Woolworth store opened in Liverpool.

The move towards motor cars, and therefore away from carriages, can be seen in the sales catalogues of Bracketts, the auctioneers. In February they sold a victoria, a brougham, a 2-wheeled and a 4-wheeled dog-cart. In April, W Hartree, Esq of Havering (in Sandown Park) "who is substituting motor cars for carriages" sold a victoria, a brougham and a wagonette-bus; all painted and fine-lined in green, with green upholstery.

Motoring was still rudimentary. When RH Williamson of Prospect Road sold his 3½ hp motor tri-car, he claimed that it had been to Cornwall and Devon many times, "and has never refused a hill". The motoring correspondents in January pondered whether the prohibition of steel-studded tyres (presumably to protect newly-tarred road surfaces) might lead to the introduction of front-wheel brakes. Joan Burslem's mother wore a dust-coat and a flat tweed hat tied on with a chiffon veil when travelling in their 1905 De Dion Bouton. The specialised clothing was necessary because the roads were gritty and extremely dusty. When selling his car, Mr Williamson also sold some of the equipment that was needed by the motorist: mackintosh motor coat, black leather apron and leather knee guards, 'holland' dust coats, 2 vices and a small grindstone, 2 pairs of goggles, a copper funnel, 2 voltmeters, springs, sparking plugs and a spare axle.

On the subject of tarring roads, the Council instructed the Borough Surveyor in March 1909, to prepare for the tarring of St John's Road, Mount Ephraim, Calverley and Grosvenor Roads during the summer. The work had to be done in fine weather - when Tonbridge High Street was tarred in June, rain mixed with the tar and sand and resulted in a sloppy surface, treacherous for cyclists and motorists.

Motoring could still be exciting. The *Illustrated London News* in January recommended trying something new:

"Motoring at night for the sheer pleasure of the thing, the eerieness, the excitement, the alertness of mind brought by the watchfulness that is so necessary... in the ever-changing light effect alone there is a never-ending fascination: under lamps and moon the road is a fairy road of fire, the trees are the trees of spirit-land – the world has become silver on black velvet."

One particular problem for motorists was that of children (boys) throwing stones. The AA encouraged the courts to deal seriously with the culprits. At Tonbridge in April, three boys were bound over for 12 months, and their parents required to pay damages of 18/6, for such an offence. An incident in August was a little more serious. A motorist in Westerham ran after the offending boy and smacked him. Three locals then attacked the motorist. At the resulting trial, the boy was discharged "on the understanding that he would get a good tanning from his father" - the men were sentenced to one month with hard labour.

March 17th saw a particularly interesting exercise in the use of motor transport. It was organised by the AA on behalf of the MOD. The idea was to test whether a battalion of troops complete with equipment could be transported quickly from London to the south coast to repel an invading army. In a way it was similar to exercises 100 years earlier when troops camped near Tunbridge Wells had practised marching down to Dover to fight off Napoleon's armies.

The story was that an enemy had invaded Hastings; that they had blown up the Sevenoaks rail tunnel, thus preventing mobilisation by train; and that a battalion of Guards needed to be moved quickly into the counter-attack. Members of the AA had volunteered the use of 286 cars, to which were added the chassis of 28 London taxis stripped down to carry guns, ammunition and other supplies. The cars were loaded up with troops from the Grenadier, Coldstream and Scots Guards at three London depots, and left from Crystal Palace at 9:30. The plan was to take the road through Sevenoaks, Tonbridge and Pembury and on to Hastings.

It all went very well. The column reached Sevenoaks at 10:45, Tonbridge 25 minutes later, and then stopped at Pembury for 20 minutes to re-group. The towns and villages along the route were decorated with bunting, and the road was lined with children waving flags. Most people from Tunbridge Wells went up to Pembury to watch - there were said to be 2 to 3,000 at the Camden Hotel - though there was also an excursion train laid on to Hastings. Fortunately most of the snow had cleared, and apart from one car catching fire on leaving Sevenoaks, there were no accidents. The troops got to Hastings by 1pm and marched into the town led by the band of the Sussex Regiment. The officers were treated to lunch at the Queens Hotel by the Hastings MP Mr Arthur du Cros.

The *Courier* reported that all of the cars were high-powered, with the latest improvements and magnificent upholstery. It described the sight of Tommies lolling back on silk cushions. *The Times*, witnessing the set-off from the London depots, thought some of the soldiers

Carr's Corner. The new (1905) vicarage for Holy Trinity is through the trees.

looked a bit-cramped - three of them occupying a back seat intended for only two, and thought them likely to suffer from the weather - unlike the drivers they were not dressed for the journey.

There were unkind comments in the House of Commons that the whole exercise had been set up by du Cros to benefit his own business interests. *The Times*, however, believed that Mr du Cros and the AA were motivated by no other feeling than patriotism. Mr du Cros' father, who had preceded him as MP for Hastings was the Chairman of the Dunlop Rubber Co., a major investor in Austin, and an agent for Mercedes and for Panhard, the French manufacturer. The family also owned the 'largest garage and motor repair works in the world' in Acton, and operated a fleet of London taxis.

Other Events in March

'Right to Work' Breakfasts

In the first week of March, the Right to Work committee provided breakfasts for nearly 120 wives and children of the unemployed at the Camden Road Methodist Church and the Albion Road Congregational Church. The *Courier* recorded that the meal was greatly appreciated, given the widespread distress and the extreme weather conditions. It reported that one of the women was suffering malnutrition. Winter was always a bad period for building workers with long periods out of work. They usually survived on their savings, by selling possessions and by credit; but this was only feasible if there had been reliable employment throughout the previous summer. This had not been the case in the summer of 1908, so by March 1909 many would have been trying to survive on a diet of bread and tea. (Earlier in the year a correspondent to the *Courier* had suggested that the poor should buy dates instead of meat. Dates and brown bread, he advised, made an excellent meal.)

The New Skating Rink

That same week the *Courier* reported that Mr Welton Dale had been refused permission by one of the ground landlords to open the proposed roller-skating rink behind the Great Hall. Mr Welton Dale said that the building would go to Southsea instead. The *Advertiser* was quite upset: "There is probably no other town in England more than Tunbridge Wells in which it is so difficult to introduce ideas which would directly tend to popularise the place and make it more acceptable to the townspeople and attractive to visitors. ... the project has had to be abandonned. It seems outrageous."

News of Lieutenant Shackleton

On 26th March the *Courier* reported the news of Lt Shackleton's achievement in planting the British flag 125 miles nearer the South Pole than ever before. It pointed out the links between him and the local area. In 1904 he had married Emily Dorman from Wadhurst, and two of his sisters were currently living in Rock Villa (ie Thackeray's House). Lt Shackleton was expected to arrive back in London in June - it was hoped that he might visit the town.

April

In which we consider:

- Hats, Corsets and Football

- 7d on the Rates

- Catholicism - Anglo and Roman

- Dreadnoughts and the Budget

- Plans for a new Skating Rink

The Edwardians wore hats. Josephine Butcher's father, a shopkeeper on the Pantiles, wore a bowler. The station-master at Paddock Wood, according to Siegfried Sassoon, wore a top-hat. The parlour-maid at Speldhurst Rectory could tell where the rector had gone by the hat that he had taken: a trilby - the village; a black trilby - Tunbridge Wells; black silk - London. Of course it was much more complicated for women. The *Advertiser* reported in January that mole-coloured hats were quite the rage amongst fashionable women, and that draped toques were replacing the huge hats that had been popular earlier in the winter. But it then further explained that big hats were still to be worn with dressy afternoon wear. Poor Mrs Spender-Clay, attending a Conservative party reception in January was dressed in the fashionable mole colour, but had to swathe her hat in orange and purple tulle (the party colours).

But hats had hidden dangers. A Mr Edwards, investigating why so many people in the late 19th century lost their hair (we speak these days of hair 'falling out', in Edwardian times it 'fell off') determined that it was due to the wearing of hats. In the past, he claimed, when people didn't wear hats, their hair had exercise and thus it was always long and luxurious. Mr Edwards patented a method of countering this effect - the Harlene Drill - and made lots of money.

That same January issue of the *Advertiser* provided a specification of the 'The Perfect Woman'. She would have the following attributes**:

Height:	5' 5"
Waist:	27"
Bust (under the arms):	34"
Bust (outside the arms):	43"
Upper arm circumference:	13"
Wrist circumference:	6"
Thigh circumference:	25"
Calf circumference:	14½"
Ankle circumference:	8"
Weight at the outside:	142lb

** The present author is fortunate enough to be married to a perfect 2008 woman. By careful comparative measurement he has determined that the Edwardian equivalent was possibly a little heavy around the hips.

We worry in 2008 about the effect on young women of the constant idealisation of the super-slim. It is not a new problem. The *Advertiser* may have claimed that a 27-inch waist was the ideal, but this was not the message presented to women by clothing manufacturers, retailers and advertisers - especially of corsets. Sarah Grand in one of her short stories published in 1908, tells of a fashionable young woman who forced herself to maintain a 19-inch waist throughout pregnancy.

One item of clothing that was not available in 1909 was the bra, which was first patented in 1913. What you could buy in 1909 was a garment shield (see right) in washable rubber, which fitted under your arm-pits in those days before anti-perspirants.

To revert to hats, Wickhams on Mount Pleasant announced their new range in April. They sympathised with their customers, perplexed by the extremely large hats that were the fashion in Paris, so they announced "a large number of MODERATELY-SIZED HATS suitable for ladies of simple English tastes".

*   *   *

The *Daily Mail* did its best to spoil Easter for Temperance supporters. On Maundy Thursday it announced that hot-cross buns were alcoholic. Tests had shown that twenty buns were the equivalent of a glass of beer. Still there was glorious weather on the Friday, Saturday and Sunday. The Tunbridge Wells Town football team played against L'Union Sportive Amicale de Paris, at the Swiss Cottage ground (Culverden Down). The visitors 'looked very smart and businesslike in white knickers and black and yellow shirts with a star on the breast'. Alas, they were defeated 4:0. Games like this against French teams were a regular feature. The Tunbridge Wells team was not impressed by the facilities in Paris for the return match. When the ball was kicked onto neighbouring land, the owner refused to return it. Having lost three balls in this way, they were obliged to call up a sergeant of gendarmes to retrieve them.

The post-card (right) was sent by a member of a visiting Belgian team who played in Tunbridge Wells on Christmas Day 1900. The following excerpt from a *Courier* report of the game shows the home supporters in an unexpected light:

"how is it such an enlightened and 'goody-goody' town as Tunbridge Wells possesses such a brutal and ignorant crowd? Staffordshire miners are gentlemen compared to them, and the former at least have the excuse of knowing the game. There is presumably some pleasure in shouting insulting remarks to players, though it says little for our fin-de-siècle refinement."

*   *   *

One reason for the unenthusiastic response to the Royal announcement may have been lingering disappointment over a 7d increase in the rates announced in March - effectively a 10% increase.

Cllr Col Bowring (ex Royal Engineer, with service in Afghanistan, Burma and China) went onto the attack:

- why was the town spending £500 on a band?;
- why did the Health Committee need £866 more for salaries?
- why did the Lighting Committee need an extra £2362 - let them get rid of a few lights.
- the Baths were a white elephant - why not let them?

Alderman Delves, long-serving Chairman of the Finance Committee defended the increase. It was the fault of the imperial (ie national) government who kept adding responsibilities onto local government without providing extra funding - in 1908 it had been medical examinations in schools. And then there was the economic recession: there had been few new houses built in Tunbridge Wells, and those had been small ones, which cost more to support than they generated in rates. Despite all this, he claimed that there were still only 4 or 5 towns with lower rates. A survey in the *Courier* supported his general argument, if not his precise figures. In a review of 90 comparable boroughs, the new rate was 14th lowest.

Few other councillors supported Bowring and he resigned in April. He was replaced by Charles Whitbourn Emson, another member of the Ratepayers League, in an uncontested election for the West Ward.

* * *

The Rev. DJ Stather Hunt was Vicar of Holy Trinity. He wrote the following apocalyptic statement in the parish magazine:

"To those who look around there is much at the present time to distract and even to dismay. Things seem dark indeed ... The political world, the social world, the spiritual world, the ecclesiastical world, all seem dark, and some of us think will grow still darker until the last and gladdest day shall break. But the present outlook is dark indeed."

What was worrying him was a report recommending the legalising of Eucharistic vestments, worn by the priest

The Rev DJ Stather Hunt

when celebrating Holy Communion. Mr Hunt's response does seem a little extreme, though his point of view had been common in 19th century Tunbridge Wells. Through most of its history the Church of England had followed sober practices with few elaborate rituals. This was challenged in the later 19th century by the enthusiasts of Anglo-Catholicism who sought to introduce vestments, candles on the altar, incense, the 'eastern position' (in which the priest faces away from the congregation). Many of these practices were not actually forbidden by the church and have since become more widely accepted, but they horrified its more protestant-minded members, who predominated in Tunbridge Wells. In 1909 the mood was tending towards tolerance, which perhaps accounts for Mr Hunt's despair.

In Tunbridge Wells those of an Anglo-Catholic persuasion were served by St Barnabas. Its consecration in 1893 had been boycotted by Canon Hoare and other clergy, but it was popular and drew a congregation from far beyond its parish. In 1909 the issue there was the introduction of plainsong by the vicar. The congregation found this too difficult and asked for Anglican tunes. The vicar replied: "I will never have Anglican tunes as a matter of principle... it is a debased taste". A visitor from St James likened the monotone plainsong *Amen* to the braying of 'a certain quadruped'.

There had been a Roman Catholic church in the town since 1838 - St Augustine's, which occupied the corner site in Grosvenor Road where Tesco now stands. The priest in 1909 was Canon James Keatinge. He was relatively new to the post, having replaced Father Charles Stapely , "tubby, bald, a grand extrovert with a superb sense of humour, who loved a good joke, a good cigar and a good whisky". One of Father Stapley's main achievements was to establish the separate parish of Tonbridge and to raise funds for a church there. The Catholic communities in both towns were quite small - a survey in 1898 had identified 313 practising Catholics between them, and most were poorer people. A rich donor was needed to fund the new church.

StAugustine's Roman Catholic Church

Mrs Hannah Fenwick, of Upper Grosvenor Road offered £5,000 for Tunbridge Wells and £2,500 for Tonbridge - enough to build Corpus Christi in Lyons Crescent. The offer came with conditions: an annuity of £350 and a mass every week of her life, plus 200 on her death, but the profligacy of the church hierarchy caused problems. The Bishop increased the annuity by £50, and promised 50 masses a year for her son. In 1902 he allowed her another £100 annuity and a further 100 masses a year. In 1903 a new bishop added a further 150 masses. As a result the new church was encumbered with commitments it found very difficult to meet. With only about 8 masses a week, there was little scope to raise the required funds to pay the annuities. Mrs Fenwick's benefaction was regarded with some bitterness for years to come.

There were elements of anti-Catholic feeling within the town. In February a meeting was held in Pembury to consider the creation of a memorial to Margery Polley - the local women burnt at the stake at the time of Queen Mary. The comments of Col Marsh, who chaired the meeting, about Catholics, led one correspondent to the *Courier* to write: "one could imagine that, had he the power, he would not leave alive one man, woman, or child professing that faith". The Polley memorial was opened in July. Col Marsh spoke of the continuing need to protect the liberties that had been bought by the sacrifices of the martyrs. Protestant Union leaflets were for sale, including: *Eighteen Reasons why I am not a Roman Catholic.*

Catholicism, and plainsong at St Barnabas, weren't the only threats. A letter to the *Advertiser* in 1908 warned about the Church of Jesus Christ of the Latter Day Saints, "one of the most pernicious forms of infidelity and blasphemy". The Mormons were seeking to draw young girls over to Utah, and were to be seen, day after day, talking with maidservants on doorsteps.

*   *   *

A *Courier* editorial of 26th March leads us into a new topic: "The position in which the country finds itself after the debates of last week is not one which should in any way give rise to panic, but it is one that makes immediate and resolute action essential ." Of course the *Courier*'s intention was very much to make its readers panic; the paper took every opportunity it could to embarass the government. In this case the debates related to the Naval Estimates.

The British, generally speaking, were proud of their army, but they were not blind to its shortcomings. But they felt secure in the knowledge that the Royal Navy, the most powerful force on earth, would protect them. In 1897 the navy had 62 battleships, 26 more than France and 50 more than Germany. The entire situation, though, was altered in 1906, with the launch of HMS Dreadnought - a new design which made existing ships obsolete, so that a numerical superiority in pre-Dreadnoughts counted for little. But still, the British ship-building industry was the best in the world - the Royal Navy could very quickly re-establish its pre-eminence.

Reginald McKenna, the First Lord of the Admiralty admitted on 16th March that this was not true: the Germans were capable of (almost) matching the British navy in the new class of battleship. To a nation accustomed to having a navy that was the equal of the next two put together, the idea of only having a slight superiority was startling. McKenna proposed the construction of four new capital ships that year, with the possibility of a further four the following year. However, there was no funding for the second four, and there was opposition from certain Liberals to even the first four.

This was the origin of the slogan "We want eight, and we won't wait", and the campaign to build all of them immediately. This was certainly the view of many in Tunbridge Wells. The East Ward Conservative Association held its annual meeting on 15th April in Camden Road. Cllr Haughton Watson spoke first and addressed this crisis in which the future of the Empire was at stake. His claim that Tunbridge Wells would demand eight Dreadnoughts with no uncertain voice was met with applause.** And a speech in Tonbridge by a Capt Osborne RN, ostensibly about Nelson, got its loudest cheers when he stated "we must go on building Dreadnoughts for all we are worth". Not just Dreadnoughts though - Capt Osborne was a great believer in the benefits of destroyers too.

One of the main opponents of increased naval expenditure was Lloyd George, the Chancellor of the Exchequer. Another, surprisingly enough given his later history, was Winston Churchill. The 1909 budget was never going to be an easy one. The Liberals had come into power with a strong social programme, and Old Age Pensions, for example, had proved far more expensive than had been estimated (no-one realised there were so many old people in Ireland). The *Courier* in February, enjoying the country's fear of what was to come in the Budget, described it as "a great industrial nation, aghast at the results of its own electoral folly". It was all the more surprising then, that in its Budget report of 30th April, the *Courier* recorded that "general satisfaction was expressed among professional and business men". The explanation seems to be that its deadlines did not allow it to hear the whole of the Chancellor's four and a half hour speech. In its entirety the 1909 Budget, the 'People's Budget' as it came to be called, was all that the *Courier* had feared. To Lloyd George it was "a war Budget ... raising money to wage implacable warfare against poverty and squalidness". The *Advertiser*, a Liberal paper, described is as "magnificent". To others it was an outrageous and deliberate attack on one political class. Its most contentious element was a tax on the unearned increase in the value of land. It was felt to be a direct attack on the power of the big landowners. Bitter fighting over the Budget was to dominate politics for the rest of the year.

** The report of this meeting went on to say that Robert Vaughan Gower, a popular local figure, was met by 'Kentish Fire' - which the Oxford Dictionary defines as an organised, prolonged and noisy applause. I suspect that the term was used mainly of less refined audiences.

Other Events in April

Prison Escape

In April, Sidney Dunn, charged with stealing old lead and brass, escaped from the cells in the police station behind the Town Hall (then situated at the corner of Calverley and Camden Roads). He squeezed between bars only 5½" apart and got out into a courtyard. He then climbed back into a different part of the Police Station, went through the back yard of the Town Hall, and out into Camden Road. According to the *Courier* "the police are moved to admiration at his agility, as much as annoyance at his self-effected release". Dunn probably knew the geography of the building quite well. In April 1908 he had been charged with two others with stripping lead from a roof in Ferndale, and it was said then that he had a previous conviction. He was re-arrested in October for stealing clothes while hop-picking, and sent to Borstal for two years**.

Education is to Blame

Earlier in the month the Mayor had spoken at a meeting in the Primitive Methodist Church in Camden Road. His subject was "crime figures calculated to humble the national complacency". Violent crime, he said, was decreasing but crime which required some degree of education and cleverness was distinctly increasing (It's not clear where he would have placed Sidney Dunn in this classification). He blamed education, which had "sharpened the mind of the once clumsy criminal". Education needed re-directing - it needed to concentrate more on the importance of God.

'Typical of Tonbridge'

That was the headline used by the *Courier* when reporting a case between two female workers at Truscott's printing works. The story involved a Mrs B accosting a MissC over a dispute at her daughter's place of work. Miss C called Mrs B a ----; Mrs B hit Miss C; Miss C pulled Mrs B's hair; Mrs B slapped Miss C and threw her in the mud. Sir William Geary, Chairman of the Bench, was at a loss to understand such behaviour. The *Courier* was being perhaps a little unkind to Tonbridge.The following encounter happened in Tunbridge Wells High Street in April. A man and his brother were walking home one evening. They came upon two young men and two young women

** At his retrial he claimed that the escape had actually been simple - a gate in the police station had been left open. The Chief Constable strongly denied this. Perhaps Dunn was just making trouble.

walking four abreast across the pavement. One of the young men brushed against him, asking 'did he want all the room?'. On remonstrating with the young men, they knocked him down. One of the young women kicked his head. The young men then offered to fight him, and the young women used obscene language.

New Roller Skating Rink Planned

The *Courier* reported that H Groves had acquired the land above the railway tunnel facing Mount Pleasant, and was proposing to erect a skating rink. The building would be called the 'Alexandra Hall', and would also be available for tennis, badminton, dances and exhibitions. It would be recognised amongst the élite as a place for afternoon rendezvous. In the meantime a Miss Lloyd organised a roller-skating carnival at the Byng Hall. Thirty members of her skating club went in fancy-dress, 'mainly women, which added to the charm - for they glided over the smooth floor with an easy grace not always achieved by gentlemen".

HMS Thunderer, one of the 1909 Dreadnoughts, the last major ship built at the Thames Ironworks, Blackwall

May

In which we consider:

- The Life of a Country Gentleman

- A Servant's Life

- Use of the Royal Prefix

- Empire Day

- Emigration

Late one afternoon in May, a young man was driving home from Tunbridge Wells in the family's new dog-cart, which was very comfortable, two-wheeled, rubber-tyred, nicely varnished, and much the same colour as brown sherry. He wasn't thinking much about the Budget, or about Dreadnoughts, or about any of the other things that young men think of. For this was Siegfried Sassoon - as those of you who have read his autobiography '*Weald of Youth*' will have realised - and he had just had his first poem published.

Sassoon was 22. He lived with his mother and brothers near Matfield. Theresa Sassoon came from an artistic family; her father did the statue of Boudicea next to Westminster Bridge, and she herself studied painting. In 1884 she married Alfred Sassoon, from an immensely rich Jewish family. Alfred's mother was upset at his marrying out of the faith, and cut him off from the family. However, he had some money from his father, so he and Theresa were able to buy Weirleigh, a nine-bedroomed house on the Paddock Wood road. They had three sons, but in 1889 Alfred left her to live with his mistress in London. He died in 1895, leaving them comfortably off, but not rich.

Theresa loved the countryside, and settled into life there, establishing a social network amongst the local gentry within a range of ten miles - the distance that could be comfortably covered by dog-cart. She also stayed in touch with her old friends thus retaining links with the artistic life in London. She may have been artistic, but she wasn't Bohemian, more of a High Anglican. She had the three boys christened at St Stephen's - the precursor to St Barnabas, just off Camden Road. She also enjoyed swimming - Sassoon talks of trips on the Medway at Wateringbury in a borrowed steam launch.

The boys were educated at home until their early teens. They were not allowed to associate with the village boys, even the sons of local farmers were considered 'unsuitable'. Sassoon was never especially academic, though the family trustees saw a future for him in the Law. After attending a crammer in Frant he went up to Cambridge, but left without taking a degree. In 1909 he had an income of about £400 a year, which was just about enough to support the life of a country gentleman. He played golf at Lamberhurst. He collected first editions. He played cricket for Blue Mantles. He was also an enthusiastic dancer, attending perhaps half-a-dozen balls each year.

Sassoon had two major passions: poetry and hunting. In 1909 he published a collection called *Sonnets and Verses*, but they were not especially good. In a way it was his hunting that led to a breakthrough with the poetry. Sassoon rode with the Eridge but also with the Southdown. In early 1912, kept indoors by bad weather, he turned out a parody of a recent Masefield poem, written in Sussex dialect. It tells the story of a farm-hand awaiting trial for murder. In this extract the narrator is lying in wait to take revenge on Bill, who has thrown him out of a pub:

> He pass'd me by, all strain'd and ready;
> Thump went my heart, but I was steady;
> I'd got the pluck that wants no bracing;
> I tripp'd him up and kicked his face in -
> Bill blinked his eyes and gave a guggle,
> And lay there stiff without a struggle **

It would be absurd to claim that this is written from any real experience as a Sussex farm-hand, but it showed that Sassoon could write from real life, and enabled family contacts to press his case to be taken seriously as a poet. Sassoon's later career as a war-hero/poet, conscientious objector, and writer, is beyond our scope, but we should make one connection. Rachel Beer, who lived at Chancellor House (see page 161) was his aunt. She was Alfred's sister, and was the only one to support him and Theresa after their marriage. Sassoon remembered her with affection from the time of his youth: "dark-haired, pale, and handsome, she always gave the impression of having slept badly the night before", but is silent on her years in Chancellor House. When she died in 1927 she left him £50,000.

When the children were young the Sassoon establishment at Weirleigh comprised: cook, scullery maid, parlourmaid, nurserymaid, gardener(s), groom and stable lad, which was typical for country gentry with no pretentions to grandeur. In an establishment of this size, the responsibilities of each role were clearly understood. There was a hierarchy and the possibility of career progression. This is demonstrated by the experience of Bessie Smith, a maid in the rectory at Brenchley (as recorded by Kirsty McLeod in *The Last Summer*). Bessie arrived from Ireland in 1910 to work in the kitchen. "I learnt as I went along. I worked my way up through the washing-up, peeling the vegetables, preparing the cooking pots." Each morning that summer she was up as soon as it was light, to clean the range and the long scrubbed kitchen table. "You put a lump of salt on it, then poured a kettle of boiling water over. That took the grease out. The floor was stone. There was no mop or anything. You got down on the

** Published as *The Daffodil Murderer* under the pseudonym Saul Kain.

Domestic staff at the home of Siegfried Sassoon, c1890. Courtesy of Elizabeth Doone, whose great grandmother, Emily Oliver (seated left) was under-nursemaid. They appear to be especially well-dressed - perhaps for the benefit of the photographer.

sack - a 'kneeler' - with a pail and brush." By 1914 she was working upstairs and being shown how to cook. Bessie was fairly unusual in being 23 when she started - 14 or 15 would have been more usual.

We also have the memoirs of Fanny Woolgar, who was employed as parlour-maid at Speldhurst Rectory in 1913 (told by Sheila Farrance in *Memories of a Village Rectory*). She was also 23, but had established herself at a higher level in the hierarchy. There were six indoor staff at Speldhurst: lady's maid, cook, house-maid, under house-maid, kitchen-maid and parlour-maid, plus a chauffeur and two garden boys. Fanny's day started at 6. She would be dressed in a white drill frock with a linen apron and dust-cap. Her responsibilities centred on the dining-room. She cleared and lay the fire, then cleaned the carpet with tea leaves and a stiff broom, and the rest of the room with a dust-pan and brush. She then took up early morning tea (prepared by the kitchen-maid) to the Rector and his wife, and hot water for him to shave. She laid out his clothes, laid breakfast for him in the dining-room, and prepared a breakfast tray for his wife. After prayers she served breakfast to the Rector and was then able to take her own breakfast. Luncheon was served at 1 o'clock. By then she had changed into a black serge dress with white apron and cap. The maids then had their dinner - their main meal of the day.

3pm was theoretically the time for visits, but, being a Rectory they were often disturbed throughout the day. Tea was at 4:30 - tiny sandwiches of very thin bread and various fillings, and scones with butter and home-made jam. Tea was served in the Library, or in the Drawing Room if there were visitors. Ladies kept their hats on at luncheon and tea. Then there was a rush to get supper ready for

7:30. Full evening dress was the rule for visitors - dress coat, white or black waistcoat, black trousers, black or white tie, patent leather boots or shoes. A dinner-jacket was acceptable for eating at home or with very close friends. Any visiting ladies would be supported by the housemaid, she (the parlour-maid) would valet the gentlemen.

The *Advertiser* provided advice for guests:
* you must never talk about the food - the hostess is supposed to have provided the best of everything,
* an occasional 'Thanks' to the servant is not amiss, but it is unnecessary to keep on expressing gratitude,
* it requires an undoubted expertness and practice for a man with a moustache to take soup in an inoffensive manner. The accomplishment is worth the trouble of acquiring.

After the evening meal there was mountains of washing-up to do, then laying up supper for the servants, and preparing the 'grog-tray' for the gentlemen. The maids were normally in bed by 10:30 or 11, though it could be after midnight if there were guests. The last task of the day was to carry the silver up to the Rector's bedroom for safe-keeping - that was the only time Fanny was allowed to use the main staircase.

There were limited facilities for personal hygiene at both rectories. At Speldhurst the servants used a hip-bath in the parlour-maid's room, which wasn't convenient and was one reason why they got through eight cooks in five years. But then very few ordinary households had bathrooms - washing was done at a wash-stand - hot water being carried up in a brass can by the servant. In the town many people would go to the public baths in Monson Road each week, where a hot bath could be had in a private room for a penny. At Brenchley, the servants used a hip-bath in the laundry. There was no lavatory, just a bucket with a lid in the garden.

Bessie Owens described how the Brenchley washer-women would come in on Mondays to boil up the clothes in a copper, and then starch them, blue them and wring them out. A similar process is described by Joan Burslem who lived in Calverley Road, Tunbridge Wells. Here the process took three days, finishing with the ironing on Wednesday. In 1901 there were 509 women in Tunbridge Wells employed in Laundries or as Washer-women (see page 70).

As a parlour-maid Fanny earned £24 a year, plus board. One shilling a week was deducted for laundry of her dresses, aprons, collars and

WASHING
WHITE
AS
SNOW

cuffs. She had to supply her own uniform, which was the standard procedure. A review of the classified adverts in the *Courier* in February 1909 suggests the following annual salaries:

Cook	£18 - £30
Parlour-Maid	£26 - £30
House-Maid	£16 - £24
Kitchen-Maid	£ 8 - £12

These are the traditional roles that would be found in households with more than one servant. Most (60%) of households, though, only had one servant, called a General, or a Cook-General. Their salaries were in the range: £14 to £20, and less, about £10, for a 'Young General' or a 'Useful Help'. Of the positions on offer in February over half were for 'Generals', many of them for work in boarding houses, and nearly half for positions in Eastbourne.

It is difficult to compare conditions in domestic service with those, say, for shopworkers - so much depended upon the character of the employer. Florence, the maid employed by Josephine Butcher's family, seemed to eat with the family, though that was probably so that she could supervise the children. Living together in a relatively small house with three small children, her relationship with the family seems a little like that of an au-pair, though she did much more work, and it is difficult to imagine an au-pair emptying the family's chamber-pots. More than 55% of female servants were under 25. It was not a role for married women, especially those with children, though there were exceptions. The lady's maid at Speldhurst, for example, had a young daughter. Arrangements had to be made for the child to live with her grandmother, the maid being allowed one night off each fortnight to visit her.

In the 1911census there were over 1.4 million 'indoor servants. Of these less than 55,000 were men. None of the adverts in the *Courier* was for a male servant, though there was one Situations Wanted advert placed by a 19 year old looking for a position as Second Footman. At 5' 8" (an essential piece of information for prospective employers, who liked their footmen to match) he was probably a little short. These figures for 'indoor servants' do not include the many male grooms, coachmen, gardeners, and chauffeurs.

The 1901 census showed a ratio of 47 indoor servants to every 100 households in Tunbridge Wells, a figure higher than the average for Kent, but lower than Beckenham, Chislehurst and Sevenoaks. A quick analysis of the 1901 census shows some typical patterns:

- Streets with virtually no servants: St James Park, Newcomen Road, Western Road, Warwick Road.
- Streets where perhaps 1 in 4 houses had one servant: York Road.
- Streets with on average 2 servants (typically a cook and housemaid): Madeira Park, St James' Road (the section described on page 6), Lansdowne Road).
- Streets with an average of 4 servants (cook, housemaid, parlourmaid, kitchenmaid), plus a coachman/gardener: Calverley Park Gardens, Hungershall Park, Nevill Park (two of the houses in Nevill Park also had a butler and footman).
- Streets where most houses had five or more indoor staff including butler and footman: Broadwater Down, Pembury Road.

*   *   *

The general public may have shown little interest in the Royal prefix, but traders were quick to respond. On 14th May, Mr Sidney Lane announced that his shop at 51 St John's Road, was to become 'The Royal Tunbridge Wells Stores'. GO Hughes of The Pantiles were advertising a souvenir silver spoon of Royal Tunbridge Wells at 6/-.

The most striking use of the title though, was a huge advertisement at Charing Cross (see over page). The name ROYAL TUNBRIDGE WELLS appeared alongside the slogans 'The Kentish Health Resort' and 'One Hour from Charing Cross'. Next to it were adverts for the Wellington Hotel and local auctioneers Carter & Banks. The Advertising Association wanted to do the same at Victoria, but needed more funds. Yet again the Courier printed a negative article on the same page. This time a complaint to Crowborough Council about advertising hoardings - that they were intensely irritating and tended to do the town harm by injuriously affecting its natural beauty. What was worse, they advertised Tunbridge Wells things which didn't benefit Crowborough in the least.

The Advertising Association claimed that the Charing Cross poster had been judged 'the best railway sign in any station in London' and arranged for railway posters to be displayed all over Britain. The Association's other success was participation at the Imperial International Exhibition at White City. Royal Tunbridge Wells was

65

'Royal Tunbridge Wells' advertisement at Charing Cross May 1909
(c) British Library Board. All Rights Reserved EW 1807

represented in a 'pavilion' of southern resorts. It was the only inland resort, and stressed its 'sylvan setting' with a picture of the Common. The Association reminded residents that there was still a balance of £20 outstanding on the fees.

*   *   *

May 24th, Queen Victoria's birthday, was Empire Day. It was a relatively recent development, dating from only 1903, and was directed essentially at children - to foster patriotism, loyalty and the ideal of service to others. It was not an official celebration - the Liberal government in particular did not approve, but was taken up by churches, schools and local bodies.

The main celebrations were in the schools. They typically involved the raising of the flag, a march-past by the children, the singing of hymns, and an address by the local vicar or other worthy. At St Marks it was the Bishop of Chichester. He said that it was a day of thanksgiving in which they thanked God for being citizens of the British Empire, for being happy English children. They were especially honoured by the presence of local resident Fanny J. Wright who, in 1908, had written the words to the Empire Hymn:

> UNFURL the Empire's Standard, and sing aloud today,
> One great glad song of triumph that echoes far away,
> "For GOD, for King, for Country," we pledge ourselves to be,
> True servants of our Empire, in strength and unity.

66

To think, to bear, to labour, to welcome duty's call,
May each by self-surrender learn fellowship with all,
"For GOD, for King, for Country," strive ever so to be,
True servants of our Empire, in love and sympathy.

The Empire's Red Cross Standard unfurled aloft to-day,
Bids every loyal subject, to work, to watch, to pray,
"For GOD, for King, for Country," that future ages see,
The servants of our Empire, heirs of Eternity. Amen

At St James School the children were told how the people of Kent
had to be ready to defend London. This was particularly relevant at
St James, where the boys could learn to shoot. At St Barnabas
Captain Campbell told the children of his experience at the Battle of
Tel el-Kebir (1882), and at St Johns there was a physical drill display.
At Christ Church school (below) (on the site recently occupied by
Safeway) the ceremony was less militaristic. Certainly, as soon as
the station clock struck eleven, they raised the flag and sang the
National Anthem, and then songs for each of the four home countries,
with Rule Britannia to represent England. But then there was 'a
very pretty ceremony' of plaiting the Maypole. All the girls taking
part wore white dresses, with sashes to match the braids that they
plaited.

Empire Day at
Christ Church
School 1909

(c) British Library
Board. All Rights
Reserved EW
1807

The children all received a tin of chocolates presented by the Mayor
(see page iv). The Mayor, suitably robed, attended each of the school
ceremonies (at Holy Trinity, Grosvenor, St Luke's, St Peter's, King
Charles, and the Royal Victoria schools, as well as those mentioned
above), plus the Childrens Ward at the General Hospital and the
Convalescent Home in Hawkenbury.

In the Magistrates Court, Mr William Smith, an 'aged flower seller' pleaded guilty to being drunk and disorderly in Calverley Road. The Chairman, Mr Wadham Elers, dismissed the charge because it was Empire Day. He did not, however, escape completely. As he left the court he was 'followed closely by the Police Court Missionary**, who administered sound advice to the old fellow'.

The emphasis during Empire Day was on strengthening ties with the colonies: Canada, New Zealand and Australia. Emigration to the colonies was seen as a useful solution to unemployment. The Tunbridge Wells Colonising Society offered assisted passages (38 in 1905, 91 in 1906, 157 in 1907). Canada was the most popular destination, though the secretary of the society admitted that they would not achieve one of their original objectives - setting up a Tunbridge Wells in Canada - as land was becoming too expensive.

An ex-farmer representing the Canadian government was in the area in March on a recruitment drive. He made himself available for four hours each evening in local hotels. It is noticeable that these were mainly in nearby villages - what Canada wanted was farmers, and female servants. The same was true for New Zealand where assisted passages were offered for farmers, agricultural labourers, shepherds and female domestic servants***. And yet there was a letter to the *Courier* from Harold Moore, who had been a sign-writer from Grove Hill Road, telling of his success, as a sign-writer, in Canada. Another letter, from AH Camforth, a former carpenter in Tunbridge Wells, told a different story. He had gone to Australia, and told of failures due to hot winds and locusts, three inches long. He called the promises of the Australian immigration authorities 'rotten to the core'. The *Courier* sent the letter to the Australian Agent General for comment. They said it was an unusual story - locusts were rare in that part of Australia, and then they pointed out that Mr Camforth had not made a great success of life in England either.

The Rev RL Gwynne wrote from Tasmania where prospects were bright and demand for skilled labout constant. He was less sanguine about South Africa where the post-war boom had ended, though Rhodesia was promising. He spoke of his experience on the immigrant ships to New Zealand. Many of the colonists were too old to adapt to the different circumstances, many were 'street-spoiled' - over-dosed on sport and gaming. Only about 20% had 'good old British grit'.

** Precursor of the Probation Officer.

*** Cost of passage to Australia/NZ - £12-16 unassisted, £2-8 assisted. To Canada £6-8. Less to US.

The rest had been 'pitch-forked anywhere, to get rid of them'. The same thing happened in Tunbridge Wells. On May 14th Sidney Lord appeared before the magistrates for exposing himself to little girls on the Common. He had previous convictions for the same offence. The Police Court Missionary, the Church Army, and a local lady had tried to help by sending him to Canada to start a new life, but he had returned. He was given a month's hard labour.

*   *   *

May 31st was Whit Monday. There was beautiful weather for a Sports Day at the Nevill Ground organised by the St John's Cycle, Motor and Athletic Club. There were gymnastic displays, and walking, running and cycling races. The most exciting events though, were the two motor cycle races. The racing was eventful, with falls, and belts slipping off, and delayed riders making up many laps to eventually win. Motor cycling was popular at St Johns. One of the members there represented the Rex motor cycle manufacturer in hill-climbs in the Midlands. The previous year AJ Sproston of the Invicta Motor Co entered the London to Edinburgh rally - 400 miles, which had to be accomplished in 22 hours (ie 18mph).

In 1903 the general speed limit was set at 20mph. There were concerns that this was too high. The general feeling in Tonbridge was that 8mph was sufficient "nobody would be so insane as to suggest a 12 mile limit". The Tunbridge Wells tradesmen came to a different conclusion - they were worried that speed limits would stifle trade.They preferred the approach adopted in Southborough, which had signs which simply requested motorists to drive slowly.

CE Bennett (with the cycle), winner of the 5-mile race at the Nevill on Whit Monday. W Hodgkinson, in the stripes, came third.
(c) British Library Board. All Rights Reserved.
EW1807

Sometimes driving slowly didn't help. Arthur Meyer was killed by a car going no more than 5 mph. The Chief Constable said that it was a very dangerous corner (at the bottom of GroveHill Road). He felt that there was a need for 'places of safety' but the Works Committee didn't like them, and " police recommendations were paid very little attention." The Mayor was not pleased with this little outburst. The following week the Chief Constable was required to retract his statement. Later in the year magistrates levied a fine of 40s for what they termed "a most dangerous and reprehensible practice". This turned out to be learning to drive in the middle of town. The luckless learner had turned into Mount Ephraim from London Road and driven straight into a horse and carriage.

Other Events in May

A cinematograph performance in the Camden Hall on 31st had to be abandoned when the film caught fire. It was immediately placed in an asbestos box and covered with sand - kept ready for such an event. The danger of fire from the highly inflammable film stock used at the time led to the Cinematograph Act of 1909. This required premises to be licensed, and led indirectly to film censorship.

Skating Rink Plans Threatened

Residents of Lonsdale Gardens, fearful of the new rink, appointed solicitors Murton Neale to protect their interests. Nothing more was heard of the scheme.

Poetic Laundry

One of the laundries had very poetic adverts. Tunbridge Wells Laundry in Market Road (see page 172) used the following verse:

'upon the Meads I met a Maid, and low in accents soft she said ... I wash for thee'

The inspiration for this seems to lie in Heine's *Book of Songs*, written in the 1820's**. The poet, in a dream, is in a garden 'wondrous fair" and comes across a maiden doing some washing:

Then to her side I made my way, And whispered low : ' Tell me, I pray,
O Maiden sweet and wondrous fair, For whom you wash that white robe there ? '
'Make ready !' straight she answered me, 'Thy winding-sheet I wash for thee ! '

It's an interesting image with which to advertise a laundry. I wonder how widely the allusion would have been recognised by prospective customers.

**An English translation was published in 1907.

Summer Days

In which we consider:

- **Leisure Activities**

- **Alienation from Modern Life**

- **The Elite**

- **Day Trippers**

- **Missionaries**

So what did they do in the evenings before television? Some of them undoubtedly went to political meetings. There was much more direct involvement in party politics, with a major speech at least once a month. And there were regular meetings of friendly society 'lodges' and temperance societies. These always seem to end with some form of musical entertainment. Even when the Cycling Club went on an evening run to

Groombridge, it concluded in a 'smoker' at the Junction Inn, with five or six members doing 'turns'.

Servants like Bessie Ellis might have spent the evening sewing or knitting, while somebody read to them, usually from Dickens. For those who preferred more recent books, EM Forster's *A Room with a View* came out in 1908, as did Arnold Bennett's *The Old Wives' Tale*. Forster had lived in Tunbridge Wells, and makes his character Cousin Charlotte a resident of St Peter's. I like to think that she attended the lectures on Florentine Art at the Town Hall in January. Both books allude to the town as being genteel and old-fashioned. Residents were perhaps more likely to have been reading the works of Marie Corelli. Her *Holy Orders, The Tragedy of a Quiet Life* was published in 1908 and was so popular that the Williams Library in Mount Ephraim Road was able to charge premium rates**.

Visitors to the rectory in Speldhurst were treated to recitals by the rector's step-daughter on the grand piano - musical evenings there were especially popular. On evenings without visitors, the rector's wife would study her stamp album, or crochet or embroider. Sometimes the rector and his wife would play cards. Bessie Ellis in Brenchley enjoyed the occasional whist-drive in the village, though whist had been supplanted by bridge amongst the fashionable set since the 1890's. In October the *Gazette* reported that a craze for jig-saw puzzles was sweeping across London.

BLOW FOOTBALL

In April, Mr RH Williamson of Prospect Road sold his Edison Home Phonograph and 3 dozen

** I haven't read it so I shouldn't really comment, but the critics accused her of purveying 'commonplace sentimentalities'.

records, for £2.12.6. 'Talking machines' had been mass-marketed since the 1890's. Mr Williamson's machine, being an Edison, probably played cylinders. The flat disk player (right) advertised by Barnard's in Camden Road, was a 'Gramophone'. It was quite an expensive hobby, Mr Williamson sold a further six sets of records (3 dozen in each) for an average of 10 shillings each set.

In May the open-air swimming baths in the Grosvenor Recreation Ground were re-opened for the summer. The pool was available throughout the year for season-ticket holders. Four of them enjoyed a dip each morning at 8am, and held a race there on Christmas Day. Earlier in the month, the Council agreed to try out women-only sessions at the indoor baths in Monson Road - 3 to 6 pm on Wednesdays. In November they considered banning smoking there. Cllr Symes in particular was concerned at "young fellows being allowed to idle their time in smoking at the baths and expectorating about the place".

In May the Culverden golf links were extended to 18 holes, and on 24th April a new bowling green opened in Grove Hill Road. The *Advertiser* praised the bowls club for being more socially inclusive than golfing clubs, where tradesmen were not wanted. In what was possibly a well-known comment at the time, it pointed out that if a man sold soap by the ton rather than the pound, or calico by the mile rather than the yard, a distinction would be made - he would be classed as a merchant, not a trader.

Speldhurst had its own form of recreation - the Rat and Sparrow Club - a society dedicated to the extermination of small animals and birds. The Club met in April to award prizes: to Mr Ashby, for 1,295 rat tails; Mr G Still, for 75 stoats' tails and 68 weasel tails; Mr O Austen for 31 bullfinches, and so on. In all they destroyed 2,707 moles, 82 jays, 56 crows, 199 bullfinches, 5,246 rats, 6,584 sparrows(or similar), 280 stoats, and 186 weasels.

These references to stoats and weasels lead naturally to *The Wind in the Willows (1908)* by Kenneth Grahame. It's the story of a water-Rat, a Mole, and a Badger, and their fight to defend the cosy, traditional world of the Riverbank against the inhabitants of the Wild Wood - weasels, stoats and ferrets. The weasels and stouts are usually said to represent the working classes, and to reflect Grahame's fear of them. The following extract, abbreviated in places, could represent a conversation between two residents of the West Ward about other parts of Tunbridge Wells:

"What lies over *there*?" asked the Mole.

"That? O, that's just the Wild Wood," said the Rat shortly, "We don't go there very much , we river-bankers."

"Aren't they - aren't they very nice people, in there?" said the Mole a trifle nervously.

"W-e-ll," replied the Rat, "let me see. The squirrels are all right ... but there are others", he explained in a hesitating sort of way. "Weasels - and stoats - and foxes - and so on. They're all right in a way - I'm very good friends with them - pass the time of day when we meet, and all that - but they break out sometimes, and then - well, you can't really trust them, and that's the fact."

It wasn't just the workers that Grahame feared; he disliked the whole modern way of life, and especially London, with " its swarming slums, its foul fogs and polluted air, its counting houses and banks, its prostitutes and gin palaces, its ceaseless noise ... the new way of life which was spreading like a cancer ". Yet Grahame wasn't some cloistered country dweller. He was Secretary to the Bank of England - its third most senior official.

Another author who disliked aspects of modern life was 'Madame Sarah Grand' who lived in Grove Hill Road. She took the name after leaving her husband, who disapproved of her feminist views. In 1908 she published *Emotional Moments*. In it she talks of her dislike of London "a stifling world, reeking of full-fed humanity, of the baser passions; a terribly hustling, jostling, over-crowded world of people all intent on securing a good place for themselves". Yet her stories do not call for social change. Certainly her strong female characters are frustrated at not having more purpose in their lives, but there is no suggestion that the maid in one story, working twice as hard as necessary because of the thoughtlessness of her mistress, will rebel, or that if she did, there would be any difficulty in replacing her. Sarah Grand's solution to the malaise which seemed to be affecting both her and Kenneth Grahame, can be found in *The Times* of 20th January. In it she describes a period of four years when she suffered from extreme debility and exhaustion. The answer was Sanatogen - taking it three times a day, she felt the benefit almost immediately.

One can understand those who found it difficult to handle the physical difficulties of London in 1909 - the noise, the bustle and the pollution. But there were also those who felt that the age was afflicted by some particular moral degeneracy. Such people exist in all periods - it seems to be a particular personality type. The Rev JH Townsend of St Mark's was an example. His parish newsletter in June 1909 started: "it has seemed to me, for a considerable time, as if we are nearing the rapids of some great national disaster." He went on to bemoan the "increasing love of ease and pleasure among our people, the growth of luxury, the dislike of work, the decay of manly independence, the clamouring to have everything provided by the state - education, food , clothing, amusement, pensions, etc".

For grumpy old men like Mr Townsend the problems always lie with other people. For others the feelings of despair turn inwards and become self-destructive. One such was Fred Fowler, a 40 year-old house-painter. His story starts, or rather it ends, in a *Courier* headline in June "Sensational Discovery in Albion Road - Man Found With His Throat Cut". The report of the inquest provides the details. His wife, Margaret, reported that he had not been well since breaking a blood vessel, and had been unemployed for some time. He had not been a temperate man, and things between them had not been good. She had taken out a summons for separation but it had not been served. Two days before the incident, though, she had left him, taking the children with her.

Mr Fowler's son had found him in his bedroom, still breathing, but with a severe wound on the side of his neck. The bedding and bed-clothes were saturated with blood. A blood-stained razor was found in the lavatory downstairs. He had apparently held his head over the lavatory pan, and cut his throat, but missed the large blood vessels otherwise death would have been immediate. Instead, he must have held the wound together and gone upstairs. In lying on the bed, his head fell back, re-opening the wound and causing blood to spurt. He died the following Tuesday. He left a note:

"I cannot bear it any longer; you will find me in the w.c. Goodbye"

(I do not wish to make light of such a document, but it would be interesting to know whether Mr Fowler really did use that semi-colon.)

*   *   *

The *Tunbridge Wells Gazette and Fashionable Visitors List,* dedicated one page each week to the 'Gazette Directory', a list of the 800 or so most prominent residents: from Abergavenny, Marquess of, down to

Mrs Yarborough Parker. But 800 is too great a number to be a real elite***. Residents knew who the real top-dogs were, and a glance at page 7 of the *Courier* would inform them of their activities.

In March for example, there were three presentations at Court. One was Lady Dorothy D'Oyly Carte, who was presented to Their Majesties by her mother the Countess of Cranbrook. The Countess wore a gown of black satin, relieved with gold embroidery edged with a piping of pale blue, and trimmed with jet. She had a train of soft blue satin draped with pale chiffon of the same tint and veiled with black embroidered net. Her daughter wore a simple Princess gown of embossed silver tissue, arranged with silver lace and old paste; and a train of silver-spangled net shimmering over a delicate shade of green silk, and fastened at the shoulder with old paste buckles.

Costume at Court was very formalised - trains for example were obligatory. The daughters wore white or silver, their mothers were allowed a little more ostentation. The newly presented debutantes were then paraded in a Season of balls and parties in search of suitable partners.

The picture, right, is actually of Ethel McLaughlin, in 1904. As a married woman she was allowed a tiara. Mrs McLaughlin was born at the Calverley Hotel in 1875: her father, William Pawley, was the owner. In June 1909 she in turn presented a Mrs Charles Norton. (The picture is taken from www.harrymclaughlin.com/album.htm, with permission.)

Attention in April switched to more masculine activities: the Eridge Steeplechases on Easter Monday. The Marquess of Abergavenny was present, looking "as hale and vigorous as ever". His son, Lord Henry Nevill, had a winner with his horse 'Northampton' . Most of those attending were local, though the Marquis Camden had a large party over from Bayham including HH Prince Victor Duleep Singh**.

*** There are approximately 8,000 entries in the Kelly's Directory for 1909, so this represents about 10% of the population.

In May the Marquess allowed two parties of visitors from Tunbridge Wells to visit Eridge - to enjoy the rhododendrons, take tea, and view the State Rooms. He clearly charmed his visitors. To the *Courier* he presented "all the old-world stately courtesy of the fine old English gentleman who plays the host in a manner which is almost a lost art outside the old nobility". There were those who had a different opinion of him. Siegfried Sassoon portrays him, in the character of Lord Dumborough, as a blustering bully***.

To most commentators of the period, the upper classes were desperate for something to do. From May until August they were supposed to be at their houses in Town (ie London), though there were frequent visits back to the country. The *Courier* tracked their movements assiduously. With June came Ascot and detailed reports of the gowns worn by the Marchioness Camden and Lady Idina Brassey on Gold Cup Day. Then there were garden parties - a particularly pleasant one at Fairlawne, home of the Cazalets, near Ightham, on 26th, following the opening of the new building at the V&A. And, of course, balls at Buckingham Palace, at least two of them in July.

The 'county' families lived in a parallel world, distinct from the day-to-day life of Tunbridge Wells, but not wholly divorced from it:

• the d'Avigdor Goldsmiths allowed the Unionist party to hold their annual fete at Somerhill,
• Viscount Hardinge attended a formal debate on Socialism in the Friendly Societies Hall in Camden Road,
• pheasants from the Marquis Camden's estate at Bayham were on sale by HJ Jones for Christmas - 1,850 were shot during a visit by the Prince of Wales.

In the background a constitutional crisis was developing, as the Conservative and Unionist peers in the House of Lords plotted to defeat Lloyd George's Budget.

*   *   *

The weather in June was awful. It wasn't just the amount of rain - 25 % above average - as its persistence. It rained on 19 days and the sunshine figures were the lowest for twenty years. At least it was fine on 16th, for a visit by 290 members of the Southend Chamber

---

** Son of the last King of Lahore. His stepmother lived in Madeira Park in the 1930's
*** In Memoirs of a Fox-Hunting Man - Sassoon's fictionalised account of his own early life.

of Commerce. They chartered the 'Yarmouth Belle' steamer to Strood, and came from there by train. On arrival they were met by the Tunbridge Wells Trades-men's Association. They walked across the Common to the Spa Hotel for a formal lunch, and were

Picture courtesy of Ian Boyle Collection.
www.simplonpc.co.uk.

then taken, by chars-a-banc, on a tour - Forest Road - Eridge Park - Groombridge - Toad Rock - and back to the Spa for a strawberry tea. They then walked back across the Common to Ye Pantiles and a glass of chalybeate water before catching the 7 o'clock train.

All very decorous. These can't have been the day-trippers that so worried the Tradesmen in 1908. What about a second group 10 days later - watermen from the Port of London, who came to the Wells every year to celebrate the monarch's birthday? They went to the George Hotel on Mount Ephraim for a convivial lunch. Then a drive, then tea , then 'harmony was indulged in' until it was time for the last train back to London.

There were similar outings from Tunbridge Wells. Staff from the

AK Baldwin

Grosvenor Printing Works in Newton Road** went to Southend for the day - by train to London Bridge and a steamer from there. They were accompanied by Mr AK Baldwin who had founded the company in 1872 , though he had handed over control to his son in 1907. His main occupation in 1909 was organising excursions, to Boulogne for example, on August 16th. It allowed eight and a half hours ashore, all for 9 shillings return. Baldwin was organising 40,000 to 50,000 holidays a year - what had originally been a hobby grew into Baldwin's Travel Agency.

*   *   *

In June the Bishop of Honduras spoke at a service at St Mark's. It was based on his experiences in central America. I have paraphrased, below, the report of his speech in the *Courier.*

**It was in Grosvenor Road until 1904 when it was demolished for an extension to the General Hospital.

"Although the negroes have produced some exceptional men, eg Mr Booker T Washington, and one or two exceptional women, yet they are children in thought and feeling; and the children's virtues and good points and attractiveness are seen in the negroes as well as their lack of forethought and preparation for the future. The negro looks to us, like children to their parents, for guidance, protection, sympathy, counsel, superintendance, discipline, control and rule."

Today the Bishop's comments would be condemned as racist, but he was just reflecting the beliefs of his audience. It is on the missionary impulse, though, rather than the racism that I prefer to dwell. It was a central part of church life at the time, and its scope was wide. At a Festival in Tonbridge, for example, there were lectures on missionary work with Chinese Women; on the South African Railways; in the Australian Bush; and in West Africa.

The missionary societies tended to specialise. The Church of England Zenana Missionary Society targetted Indian women - 'zenana' meaning the segregated part of an Indian house. Its original purpose had been to counter the effect of Indian women in preventing Indian men from converting to Christianity. By 1909 it was concentrating on medical services, and training Indian women to be doctors. In 1908 the Tunbridge Wells branch raised £500 for this work.

The missionary impulse can be seen as just a form of cultural imperialism. It could equally be considered as a desire to share something precious with other people. And mission didn't just apply on a global scale - there were missions to the poorer parts of England. The parishioners of St Barnabas and St James, for example, supported one such mission in East London. I particularly like the Mission to French-Speaking Foreigners in London. A fund-raising lecture for this society was given - in French - in the Holy Trinity Parish Room in Goods Station Road in October.

One missionary who would have been known to many in Tunbridge Wells was Joseph Hoare, youngest son of Canon Edward Hoare - for forty years vicar of Holy Trinity. After serving his father for a short period as curate, Joseph spent twenty five years in China training local evangelists. In 1898 he was appointed Bishop of Victoria (Hong Kong) but continued his missionary work.

Bishop J. C. Hoare

79

In 1906 his younger son, 'Ted', aged 9, was sent to England to school. It was part of the way of life of many British families living overseas. Some of the letters sent by his parents have survived. The first letter from his father, in February, urged the boy to work well, play well, make friends, to try in all things to please God. In June he wrote again, sending him something for his 10th birthday. On 12th September his mother wrote, wondering what games he would be playing in the Christmas term, and telling of day-to-day events back in Hong Kong- a green snake being caught in their chicken-house. She mentioned that his father was to go off to the mainland for a week's tour with four students, and hoped that they would not be attacked by pirates. She sent another letter on 17th, describing a school treat for local children. On the envelope she added a note that a typhoon was raging. Then on 21st September she sent a quite heart-breaking letter explaining that the returning boat was destroyed in the storm, the bishop and the four students lost. She tried to comfort the boy:

"Oh my darling little Ted, Mother's heart is nearly broken, but she knows that God has done just what is really best for Father & really best for us all, though we cannot see how. You will never forget Father, will you, and how he loved you, and used to be so happy with us all. And you must remember what a dear good, noble Father, God gave you, and ask God to help you to grow up to be a good man like him."

The Bishop's body was never found. After a memorial service at the cathedral, his wife and four daughters returned to England. In June 1909 part of the mast of the wrecked boat was displayed at a Missionary Exhibition in Islington, alongside memorials to Dr Livingstone, General Gordon and HM Stanley. In November a memorial to him was unveiled in the Chapel of Tonbridge School. Unfortunately it seems to have been destroyed in the 1988 fire.

*　　　　*　　　　*

In May Mr Sidney Lane had taken to calling his shop 'The Royal Tunbridge Wells Stores'. A Mr Hollands, nurseryman of St John's Road (see page 178) was a little more circumspect. He employed a solicitor, Walter Brook, to write to the Home Office for permission to call his business 'The Royal Tunbridge Wells Horticultural Establishment'. The initial view in the Home Office was that calling a shop 'The Royal Tunbridge Wells Grocery Store' was no different from calling one 'The Portsmouth Grocery Store', or the 'Royal Engineers Yacht Club', and they were inclined to approve the request.

Then a more senior official questioned whether the King had ever intended the word 'Royal' to be part of the name of the town, and therefore available for use by tradesmen. It seems quite possible that he thought he was dealing with a spa building - like the Royal Baths in Harrogate. The official suggested that adopting the formula 'Royal Borough of Tunbridge Wells' would get around the problem, but was told that it was too late to consider this. So they concocted a response which explained that the Royal prefix applied collectively to the town, and was not to be used for individual enterprises. It seems unlikely

that the designation 'Royal Borough' would have been approved anyway. In 1935 the Home Office corrected the General Register Office for using such a term for Tunbridge Wells in a census report.

By early June other traders were using the title: 'The Royal Tunbridge Wells Modern Machine Bakery' in Western Road for example. The owner insisted that Mr Brook check again with the Home Office. This time the reply was fast and unequivocal.

Other Events in June

Tonbridge Cricket Week

June 14th to 18th was Cricket Week in Tonbridge. One of the highlights was the Venetian Fete, held on the River Medway. The reporters from *Society* was impressed: "Wednesday night. What glories! A night of nights. Crowds line the banks, their faces bathed in rich warm flickering colours. A thousand voices join hands with the laughter of the awakened waters. Boat after boat, crowded with joyous merry-makers, swirls past. Swaying Chinese lanterns cause a kaleidoscopic effect upon the proud bosom of the river. A rocket soars skywards and splits the still warm air ..." and so on.

Take-over of the Pump Room

In June liquidators were appointed to wind-up the company which had been running the Pump Room for the last 20 years. Led by WH Delves and HC Groves it had become a moribund concern. Mr Welton Dale of the Opera House was to take over. The building would be run as a high-class resort under his personal management. Both local newspapers supported the change. There was a suggestion that it might be suitable for roller-skating.

The Carthorse Procession

In late June the Council arranged a competition amongst the staff at North Farm who looked after its carthorses. The horses were led in procession along Upper Grosvenor Road, Camden Road and Lansdowne Road to the Town Hall, where prizes were presented. The winner received a tea-pot and 10 shillings. The runners-up were given other strangely domestic gifts: a tea service and tray, cruet, and three shirts. The horses then processed via Mount Ephraim to the High Street and back by way of Mount Pleasant.

Events in Upper Grosvenor Road

William Tupper was fined 10s for accosting a young lady in Upper Grosvenor Road. After a number of previous complaints, DS Kingston had taken watch. He had witnessed Tupper go up to Edith E., say "Good Evening, Maud", put his arm around her waist and kiss her, then make several rude suggestions.

July

In which we consider:

- Cricket Week and the New Skating Rink

- Holidays in Switzerland

- Louis Bleriot and Frank McClean

- Dreadnoughts (again)

In a sense the 'season' began on 21st June, with the opening concert of the Band Season; but it was Cricket Week that dominated the summer. The previous year it had been a disaster - it had rained nearly all week. The weather wasn't the only concern - other parts of the county felt that Tunbridge Wells did not deserve a Cricket Week - that it would be more appreciated elsewhere.

Things did not start well, with disagreements between the two main organising bodies: the Cricket Week Amusement Committee and the Corporation Band Committee. Neither was officially part of the Council, though the Band Committee was given a budget by the Council to organise entertainments throughout the season. Both were keen to make a financial success after the difficulties in 1908, and both sought to maximise their income from Cricket Week. In February, the Amusement Committee offered to hire the band from the Band Committee, to play at the Nevill Ground for four afternoons, but indicated that it was going to hold its own events in the evenings. That was not acceptable to the Band Committee.

On March 6th the Amusement Committee offered to take on the band for the whole of Cricket Week, and to pay the Band Committee up to 50% of the net profits arising from all entertainments that week (other than the cricket itself). The Band Committee rejected the proposal emphasising that it had sole right to put on entertainments on the Pantiles and Mount Sion Grove. On March 23rd the Amusement Committee stated that it would not use the Corporation band at all, and approached the owners of the Calverley Grounds for permission to put on events there. On April 7th it presented a formal Resolution to the Council complaining about the Band Committee, and claiming exclusive rights to put on events in the Grove during Cricket Week.

Eventually the Mayor arranged a face-saving compromise: a Joint Committee was formed to arrange entertainments during Cricket Week, with the income split equally between the two parties. Things then went more smoothly. The Council confirmed the allocation of £500 to the Band Committee, and the Committee engaged the Bayreuth Orchestra for the season. It also hired the rival 'Ceylon Band' for a series of evening concerts in the Grosvenor Recreation Ground.

By early July the arrangements had been finalised (see opposite). The entertainments in the Grove were an innovation, replacing the traditional pierrot-type show. They were described by the *Courier* as

Monday July 12th
- Cricket vs Derbyshire at the Nevill. Bayreuth Orchestra.
- Illuminated Promenade Concert on the Pantiles 7:30 - 10:00
- Vaudeville Entertainments in Mount Sion Grove 7:00 and 8:45
- Amateur Theatricals at the Opera House 8:30

Tuesday:
- Cricket vs Derbyshire at the Nevill. Ashford Railways Works Band.
- Illuminated Promenade Concert on the Pantiles 7:30 - 10:00
- Vaudeville Entertainments in Mount Sion Grove 7:00 and 8:45
- Amateur Theatricals at the Opera House 8:30

Wednesday:
- Cricket vs Derbyshire at the Nevill.
- Vaudeville Entertainments in Mount Sion Grove 7:00 and 8:45
- Grand Illuminated Promenade Concert and Fireworks in the Calverley Grounds 7:30
- Illuminated Concert at the Spa Hotel**

Special late trains to Sevenoaks, Frant, Wadhurst and Robertsbridge.

Thursday:
- Cricket vs Sussex at the Nevill. Bayreuth Orchestra.
- Illuminated Promenade Concert on the Pantiles 7:30 - 10:00
- Vaudeville Entertainments in Mount Sion Grove 7:00 and 8:45
- Illuminated Concert at the Spa Hotel**

Friday:
- Cricket vs Sussex at the Nevill. Ashford Railways Works Band.
- Illuminated Promenade Concert on the Pantiles 7:30 - 10:00
- Vaudeville Entertainments in Mount Sion Grove 7:00 and 8:45
- Subscription Ball at the Spa Hotel

Saturday:
- Cricket vs Sussex at the Nevill.
- Illuminated Promenade Concert on the Pantiles 7:30 - 10:00
- Vaudeville Entertainments in Mount Sion Grove 7:00 and 8:45

** These were not part of the formal Cricket Week programme, but were arranged to coincide.

'experimental vaudeville', 'of the Continental type - one could imagine oneself in Paris or Berlin'. They actually seem rather tame:

The Opera House Orchestra
Mr R Tattersall - ventriloquist and conjurer
The 'Czar's Royal Dancers'
An orchestral interlude
The Roma Trio - 'three muscular and elastic performers' (acrobats)

After the event the *Courier* commented that something had to be done about getting a proper enclosure for the Grove - for every paying customer, a dozen or more simply stood outside and watched. The same problem applied to the Pantiles. There was praise for the concerts themselves: 'of exceptionally refined character' - a mixture of music from the great masters, and lighter, more recent pieces.

There had originally been doubts about the concert in the Calverley Grounds, but it was a great success: "a prettier or more acceptable form of summer evening amusement has rarely been provided for the edification of Tunbridge Wells people." It took the form of a 'cafe chantant' with the Bayreuth Orchestra (see below) providing the music. After the music there was a firework display, including tableaux of the King and Queen, and six magnesium balloons discharging coloured fire and rockets. One of these landed on a nearby roof, though there doesn't seem to have been any damage. The event was so successful, with an audience of over 5,000, that it was repeated on the Saturday.

The Cricket Week Ball had to be held at the Spa Hotel rather than the Pump Room as this was being used for other purposes (see page 94). It had some very splendid-sounding patronesses: The Marchioness Camden, The Viscountess Hardinge, Mrs Spender Clay,

The Bayreuth Orchestra

and Lady Henry Nevill. In the event none of the aristocracy attended - they were all at a State Ball in Buckingham Palace that evening. But 300 others turned up, and the local press made the best of things. *Society* said that one imagined that one was far away from England - in some Southern spot instead. It is interesting that both *Society* and *Courier* used this same definition of a successful event - that it made the participants feel as though they were abroad - England may have been powerful, dependable and important, but it lacked romance and culture.

New in 1909, and inspired perhaps by a similar event in Tonbridge, was a competition for the best-decorated premises. The winners were Semple Bros, butchers in Calverley Road which had "an appearance of delicate and fullsome prettiness"; and Biggs, the wine merchant in the Pantiles, who had decorated his shop with artificial foliage and roses, baskets of flowers and chinese lanterns. The competition brought out crowds of sight-seers, with detailed shop-by-shop descriptions in both local newspapers. Mount Pleasant and the High Street were considered the best - worthy of a royal visit - the Pantiles was a disappointment. It wasn't just the local traders who were involved - the banks in the High Street were decorated too. The emphasis in the programme on 'illuminated' events is important - decoration with coloured electric lights was all part of the thrill, especially for the event in the Calverley Grounds.

It is unfortunate that there are no pictures of good enough quality to illustrate the concerts and other events. There is a danger that we therefore associate Cricket Week with just cricket, yet this was only the pretext for a week of general entertainment. The cricket though was successful - the Kent team having improved since its failures at Tonbridge in June. In the first game they beat Derbyshire, but the victory was a little too emphatic - the game was over in two days, which meant that there was no play

The 1909 Kent team. DW Carr seated, 2nd from right

on Wednesday. The second match, against Sussex, ended in a draw, affected by rain on the Saturday. Kent went on to win the county championship that year. They had a new bowler, DW Carr (aged 37), who got a lot of attention, having mastered the new art of the googly. His father lived in Molyneux Park. Unfortunately, Carr did not play in the games at the Nevill. Despite the rain, the Cricket Week Committee was able to declare a surplus of £121.

* * *

On 7th July the Horticultural Society held its 51st annual Flower Show in the Great Hall. They had a Royal Marine band from Chatham. Unfortunately it was one of the stormiest and wettest days of the summer. Apparently this was traditional for the Flower Show. On the 18th there was the annual Hospital Sunday procession - this was more successful and is described in the chapter on August. From the 26th to 31st, there was a tennis tournament at the Nevill ground. The weather was poor and spectators few.

The Agricultural Show was on 22nd and 23rd. For two days beforehand, bulls, and pigs, and prancing horses, had been arriving at the two stations, to be driven or walked to the show-ground, a large open area where the Showfields estate is now. There was a slight decline in the number of entries, mainly in the classes for smaller animals. Although most people went to see the cattle and horses, where the prizes were won by the large local estates, well over half the entries were actually poultry, pigeons and rabbits. There were classes too for home-made bread, and butter. Mrs MA Beale of Tunbridge Wells took the prize for the best white loaf; Mrs Cane of Cousley Wood for the best wholemeal.

There was a noticeable reduction in the number of horses in the hackney and harness sections. A report by the organisers in 1908 had identified a similar fall, due to the increase in motor transport, but had gone on to say, rather optimistically: "it is impossible to believe that the horse ... can be permanently displaced. The prevalent desire for speed, always accompanied by discomfort and risk may be expected to abate, and horses will then return to favour."

There was no evidence of horses returning to favour in 1909. The number of motor cars used by the exhibitors themselves demonstrated that. After having been stable for the previous three years, the number of spectators fell in 1909, by about 11%, to 11,431.

* * *

At the end of July Mr Elvy Robb and his wife left town for Switzerland. It was a popular summer destination for the wealthier residents. The Rev WAH Legg of Emmanuel went there too. He was away for three weeks - his congregation were advised that letters would not be forwarded. The Rev RW Usher of the Baptist Tabernacle in Calverley Road joined them, on doctor's orders - for two months. Elvy Robb's destination was the Lower Engadine in the south-east of the country. It was a favourite area for another Tunbridge Wells resident - Mr Thomas Fothergill of 7 Calverley Park Gardens.

Like many a genteel resident of the town, Fothergill was a beneficiary of the industrialisation which had transformed Britain a century earlier. His grandfather and uncle had been iron-masters in the Cynon Valley in South Wales. His elder brother had followed them into the business, but Thomas had had to retire, for health reasons, aged 24. He and his wife, Laura, from another great iron-making family - the Crawshays, travelled on the Continent instead. They lived for a while on Mount Ephraim in the 1870's, but then went back to France and Italy, only returning in 1890.

Fothergill was an earnest worker for Christianity and had been a friend of Canon Hoare. He conducted services in common lodging houses and the General Hospital on Sunday evenings, and was a frequent visitor to the Workhouse. In his work as a District Visitor to Golding Street, he was a favourite with the children as he always took them sweets, and was courteous and tactful when distributing tracts to their parents. He was also an ardent supporter of the Temperance movement, and of the YMCA. Mrs Fothergill did her bit too, fund-raising for the Home for Aged Women in Bayhall Road.

Mr and Mrs Fothergill visited Switzerland every year. Their favourite was Pontresina, which is near St Moritz. He collected wild Alpine plants, and spent the winters mounting them on cards to be given to hospitals. He invented a new way of pressing flowers - using cotton-wool instead of blotting paper - which retained more of the colour. For nine years he won first prize at the All Switzerland Amateur Flower Show in St Moritz. He would frequently walk up to twenty miles in a day in the mountains - carrying tracts in French, Swiss and Italian, in case the opportunity arose to do some evangelising.

On July 21st he set off to walk to the Tschierva Hut near the Roseg Glacier with Rev Dr Grey, the British chaplain. He had complained of indigestion at breakfast which he blamed on almond cake, and

ALLED FROM HERE SUDDENLY
FOR HIGHER SERVICE
21ST JULY 1909

THOMAS
ROWLAND FOTHERGILL
OF TUNBRIDGE WELLS.ENGLAND

BE YE ALSO READY

BELIEVE ON THE
LORD JESUS CHRIST
AND THOU SHALT BE SAVED.

HIM THAT COMETH UNTO ME
I WILL IN NO WISE CAST OUT.

Picture thanks to Silvio Caflisch

had taken some ginger to settle it. After just over a mile though, he complained again of indigestion and then just toppled forward and died of a heart attack. A memorial service was held for him in Pontresina, but his body was brought back for a funeral and burial in Tunbridge Wells on the 28th.

A memorial stone (see right) was erected to Fothergill in the Roseg Valley. It survived for ninety nine years, but by early July 2008 it had split apart. The pieces were disposed of by a tidy-minded local authority.

*   *   *

July 25th is another 1909 date that has a significance way beyond the year itself - on that day Louis Bleriot became the first person to fly across the Channel in a heavier-than-air machine. It was not a wholly unexpected event - Bleriot was competing for a £1,000 prize set by the *Daily Mail*. His rival, Hubert Latham, had made an attempt six days earlier, but managed only 7 miles and had to be rescued from the Channel. It had only been five and a half years since the first ever flight, by Wilbur and Orville Wright at Kitty Hawk. Aviation, like the motor car, was developing very quickly. A Tunbridge Wells man, Frank K McClean, played an important role.

Like Fothergill, McClean was a beneficiary of Britain's industrial heritage. His grandfather, John Robinson McClean, was a civil engineer who ended up as owner of railway and water companies in the North Midlands, and of the Cannock Chase Colliery Co. Frank's father also trained as an engineer. He bought Ferncliff, in Pembury Road and built an observatory in the garden. In 1884 he moved to Rusthall House.

Francis Kennedy McClean was born in 1876. He trained as a civil engineer but when his father died in 1904 leaving over £300,000, he was able to concentrate on his private interests. One of these was ballooning. In October 1909 he was the only British entrant in the international

Frank McClean

90

Gordon-Bennet balloon race**. Twenty balloons left Zurich at about 3pm. Heavy rain forced McClean to land at 10:27 the following morning. He had reached Bohemia. The eventual winner flew for 35 hours and got as far as Poland.

In December 1908 McClean was taken for a demonstration flight by Wilbur Wright. He determined to support the development of aircraft manufacturing in Britain. The Short brothers, who were balloon manufacturers, had a licence to use the Wright brothers design. In early 1909 part of a golf course was bought at Leysdown on the Isle of Sheppey. McClean paid for it to be converted for use by Shorts. It is now recognised as the first aircraft manufacturing site in Britain.

In May the Wright brothers visited Leysdown. There is a picture of them, with the Short brothers, JTC Moore-Brabazon (first British pilot to fly in Britain), CS Rolls - and Frank McClean (standing, in the centre). In November McClean bought more land on Sheppey and gave it to the Aero Club of Great Britain. This became Eastchurch airfield.

Meeting at Leysdown May 1909

McClean himself learnt to fly in 1910, receiving certificate no 21. In 1912, he flew up the Thames from Sheppey to Westminster in a 'hydro-aeroplane' - flying under London, Southwark, Blackfriars and Waterloo bridges. In passing through Tower Bridge on his return he hit something and came down on the river. The aircraft suffered the indignity of being returned to Sheppey on a horse-drawn trolley.

In September 1909, the Advertising Association, considered arranging a flying competition between Rusthall and Crowborough. Nothing came of the idea.

*   *   *

I was very disappointed when reading the *Courier* of February 19th. I thought I had found an original 'Disgusted of Tunbridge Wells' letter. It was certainly signed 'Disgusted', but the address was

** I don't have definite confirmation that the McClean in this race was the McClean from Rusthall, but it seems likely.

Rusthall. What was upsetting Disgusted of Rusthall was the playing of football on Sundays. "it is time that all who disapprove of such things should take action." The subject of Sunday observance and falling church attendances was addressed later by the Ven Archdeacon AT Scott, of St James'. He said that the English Sunday had played an important part in making England the great and powerful nation that it was. Rather surprisingly he then went on to say that, although it needed to be a day of rest, it was more important that it was a day of change: "the weekend party at the country house, the dinner-party at the London hotel, the motor-car and the golf-links". He may even have included football in Rusthall had it occured to him.

Tonbridge Council didn't agree with the Archdeacon. They tried to introduce regulations to prevent residents from working on their allotments on Sundays. The proposal attracted derision in the national press. It was probably this that triggered the following outburst from *Society*: "I refer to Sabbath observers and their ranting piffle. When oh when will the world think for itself and annihilate narrow mindedness." By August some councillors were finding the publicity embarassing, and moved to rescind the resolution.

Sunday obviously was different. Joan Burslem remembered it as a day for visiting the cemetery - the buses there were always full. But even here, there were those whose sensitivities could be upset. Luke Pearce wrote of people coming to the cemetery to put flowers on graves, "a few are fetching water ... to freshen up drooping flowers, as though they could not possibly do that on another day". He then added: "Perhaps they can't."

Perhaps it was just football that Disgusted didn't like. He would not have been alone. Colonel Warde, MP for Mid-Kent, suggested that inter-county military sports would be a much worthier pastime. The Rev Hales from Chatham spoke at a special service for sportsmen. He described himself as being a great enthusiast, but was critical of football, especially the behaviour of the professionals: "A great deal of their leisure many of them spend in gambling, and in some instances, drinking - not all, but many are thus affected."

Tunbridge Wells had a professional football team, the Rangers. They had done very well in the Kent Senior Cup reaching the semi-final against Maidstone. Their performance in the South Eastern League was less satisfactory. They finished second from bottom and were not re-elected for the 1909/10 season. The *Tonbridge Free Press* saw little prospect of them surviving. Things got worse in June. They owed their ground landlord £40, so bailiffs took possession of the club's property: the grandstand, seating, bits of timber, and eight sheep, presumably used to cut the grass. At a bad-tempered auction, full of "unpleasant jeers and derogatory ejaculations", £34.7s was raised, including £5.10s for the sheep. The ground was at Combley Park, just north of the St Johns Recreation Ground.

At the club AGM in July, the Financial Secretary explained that they owed £130. Gate money had fallen in three years, from £801 to £460. He suggested the club was moving towards dissolution, but shareholders were unwilling to accept the advice. At a further meeting in August, the Secretary said that it was hopeless: they had no ground, no fixtures, no matches and no players. Still the shareholders refused to accept dissolution. Two in particular, Messrs Dickinson and Farmer (butchers in St John's Road and owners of the sheep), provided additional support. At the start of the new season, the team "a professional club being run on amateur lines" played its first match at a new ground near the 'Cross Keys'. Three hundred came. They lost 4 - 0 to Chesham.

Other Events in July

Imperial Maritime League

The issue of the Dreadnoughts had not gone away. A meeting was held at the Opera House in late June to form a local branch of the Imperial Maritime League. In line with the Tunbridge Wells ex-army officer stereotype, the audience contained ten Colonels. The tenor of the meeting was true to the stereotype:

* it denounced the present Government for betraying the nation,
* it demanded restoration of the two-power standard,
* it urged the House of Lords to throw out the Budget, and save the nation.

To cheers from the audience, a speaker denounced "stupid Ministers, elected by a stupid electorate". He went on: "if we are to continue to dominate the world, we need to preserve our stock …it is not preserved by the incessant immigration into London of the riff-raff of Europe, and the continuous emigration out of Liverpool of the best of our agricultural stock". Further applause. The meeting ended with 'Land of Hope and Glory' and the National Anthem.

The government organised a Great Naval Display in July, to persuade the public that the Royal Navy was still powerful - 149 fighting ships in the Thames from Westminster down to Southend. Baldwins advertised half-day trips to see them. Eventually though, the government accepted defeat, and announced on 26th July that all eight Dreadnoughts would be started within the year.

New Skating Rink

After 25 years, the town gained a new skating rink. Mr Welton Dale's transformation of the Pump Room was declared an enormous success. Morning and afternoon sessions, at 1s, were expected to be most popular with local 'society'. The evening session cost 6d. Skate hire was an extra 6d. The world champion trick skater, Valosky, was recruited to give exhibitions. On 9th July they held a Skating Carnival with fancy dress competition. Prizes went to Miss Hook of Holland, and to a gentleman dressed as a Cavalier. Valosky gave demonstrations including vaulting over nine rows of seats. The following Tuesday a Mr Percy Perfect** of Tonbridge broke his ankle while skating.

The Impact of the Childrens Act

The Children's Act came into force in April. It changed the court system for children, it forbade cigarette smoking under 16, and banned children under 14 from entering pubs***.
Sidney Wood of Golden Green was a bargeman. On Saturday afternoon July 31st, he took his six year-old son into Tonbridge, on the barge, to buy him some new boots. When they had finished he popped into the Castle Hotel for a drink, leaving his son outside. When he came out of the pub twenty minutes later the boy was gone. He looked for him on the barge, then assumed that he had gone home to Golden Green. The worried father walked back into Tonbridge three times that night looking for him. The boy's body was found later in the Medway. The inquest jury blamed the Children's Act.

** There is no-one of this name in the Kelly's directory for 1909.

*** It also raised the minimum age for executions. Children under the age of 16 could no longer be hanged.

August

Queens Grove, on the Common,
Royal Tunbridge Wells.

In which we consider:

- **Hospitals and Health**

- **Postmen, Policemen and Shop Assistants**

- **The Visitors**

July 18th was Hospital Sunday, or, more formally, the Annual Church Parade of the Tunbridge Wells Friendly Societies and Fire Brigades - another excuse for a procession. It started at the Friendly Societies Hall, went along Camden Road, Beulah Road, Lansdowne, Calverley and Monson Roads, and then via Mount Pleasant and the High Street to the Vale Royal Methodist Church. There were bands, banners and decorated carts. It was led by bands of the Royal West Kent Regiment and the Fire Brigade but most of the twenty six groups were Friendly or Temperance Societies: the OddFellows, Foresters, Gardeners, Druids, Comical Fellows, Good Templars and Rechabites. The Boy Scouts took part for the first time.

The purpose was to raise money for local hospitals. Various techniques were used. Joan Burslem remembered men with long metal tubes collecting from upper storey windows, and her delight as a child in hearing the pennies rattle down them. There were two 'hospital dogs' with collecting boxes. The weather was perfect for the 10,000 spectators lining the streets and on the Common. The Mayor led the service in the Vale Royal church. The Salvation Army handled the overflow outside on the Common, supported by the Crowborough Brass Band. Afterwards, the procession continued: Mount Ephraim, St Johns Road, Queen's Road and back to Calverley Road. In the evening there was a sacred concert in the Grove. The Bayreuth Orchestra played pieces by Mendelssohn, Gounod and Schubert; and selections from 'Lohengrin'. The concert ended with the singing of 'Abide with Me'.

They raised £168.3s. Most of it went to the three hospitals - see below - with smaller sums to the Surgical Aid Society, the District

Members of the Druids Friendly Society with decorated van

Nursing Association, and the Home for Little Incurables in Park Road.

The General Hospital was on the eastern side of Grosvenor Road, occupying the block between Good Station Road and Upper Grosvenor Road. The main building, to the left (see below), had been there since 1842, though had been much extended. The plainer building, on the corner where the Post Office is now, was built in 1904. The average number of in-patients across the year was about 57. Length of stay was much longer than now. Of the 774 in-patients over the previous year, 69 stayed for more than two months. There were some 500 out-patient attendances each week.

The
General
Hospital

The Homeopathic Hospital, on its present site, opened in 1903, though there had been a homeopathic dispensary at various sites around the town since the 1860's. It had beds for about 10 in-patients. In 1908 there were a total of 104 in-patients, 7585 outpatient attendances, and over 6000 home visits.

The Eye and Ear Hospital was in Mount Sion, in Fairlawn House. In 1908 it had 312 in-patients, and 7555 out-patient attendances. 301 operations were performed, 180 of them with general anaesthetic.

All three hospitals were voluntary organisations, supported by subscriptions and donations. The annual income for the General Hospital for 1908 came from:

Subscriptions	£1,309
Donations	£606
Hospital Sunday (and similar)	£340
Investments	£1,417
Church Collections	£410
Legacies	£1,495

The Children's Ward of the General Hospital.

An annual subscription would entitle the subscriber to attend a certain number of times as in-patient and as out-patient. This entitlement was transferrable in the form of the 'hospital letter', so that wealthy, and healthy, patrons could send along their servants, employees, or others unable to afford their own subscriptions. A letter to the *Courier* in November, for example, appealed for 'spare letters' for the poor of High Brooms. Those unable to afford their own subscription might contribute to a Friendly Society, which took out what were effectively bulk subscriptions for their members. Weekly subscriptions were about 2d. The money collected during Hospital Sunday, and on Hospital Saturdays later in the year, entitled the organisers to additional hospital letters - to be used for the benefit of anybody in need.

The hospitals also benefited from gifts in kind - regularly listed in the local papers. These would typically be magazines, or flowers and vegetables, or old linen, but there were sometimes items of specific medical use: cradles, splints, children's nightdresses.

*   *   *

The Medical Officer of Health was a council official whose responsibility was to act against the spread of infectious diseases. In 1909 there were seven deaths from measles - six children and one adult. There were two deaths from scarlet fever, three from whooping cough and three from diphtheria. In the days before vaccination, there was little that the MOH could do but isolate those affected. In December 1908 he closed St Mark's School for two weeks after an outbreak of roteln (German measles), and St Luke's for two weeks in March because of measles.

A particular concern was scarlet fever. Headteachers were urged to exclude any children with sore throats or nasal discharge and peeling skin. One mother was fined 10s in April, for 'exposing a child' in the 'peeling' stage of the disease. Those who did catch it were taken to the Isolation Hospital, in Benhall Mill Road. There were 48 beds there for scarlet fever patients, and six for diphtheria. During 1909 there were 157 and 11 cases respectively. The MOH also had access to the Dislingbury isolation hospital at Capel, shared with Tonbridge and other local authorities. It was specifically for cases of smallpox and plague. The most recent incidence of smallpox had been in 1903.

Perhaps the MOH for Tunbridge Wells had a particularly officious manner, or perhaps he was unusually conscientious, but he seems to have upset many of the neighbouring councils. In March Tonbridge Council agreed with its own MOH that he need not supply Tunbridge Wells with details of their scarlet fever cases. They saw no good coming from giving information to "an irresponsible officer in an adjoining area". In April there was an angry response from the East Sussex MOH to a suggestion that scarlet fever in Tunbridge Wells had come from children in Ticehurst. The MOH had examined the children with a powerful lens, and had found them to be simply suffering from measles. In 1908 there had been similar complaints from Uckfield.

Each year the MOH compiled statistics on health in the area. Tunbridge Wells was especially proud of its low death rates - this formed a prominent part of its advertising. The infant mortality figures were especially good for 1909 at 59/1000 (the average for England and Wales was 109). The MOH had hopes of reducing them further: "I venture to hope that no effort will be spared to educate the poorer classes ... upon the duties of motherhood and the hygiene of infant life". He drew attention to recent research on the part played by the house fly in the spread of disease. The theory of germs as carriers of disease was still relatively new, and caused some concerns. The Borough Education Committee in May decided to stop using slates, in case they carried infections. In 1908 the *Advertiser* warned of the danger of licking stamps. It was much easier and safer to lick the corner of the envelope, or wet it with the finger tips and water. And the *Daily Mail*, in a campaign against national insurance, claimed there was a threat of diphtheria from sticking the stamps on cards.

With all this uncertainty about disease and the limitations of official medecine, the field was open to unofficial cures. The adverts for such products, often claiming to tell the story of a particular patient give us an idea of what it was like to be ill in those days. Take Mr AR Burford of Rochester, for example, who cut his leg at work. Blood poisoning set in, and he had to have the leg amputated. For six weeks he lay helpless, his mother nursing him night and day. Abscesses formed all over his body eating into his bones. The doctors told him that there was nothing that they could do - it was just a matter of time. But he then took Dr Williams Pink Pills for Pale People, and was cured. Then there was the story of Miss M Russell of Bradford. She had fallen victim to extreme languor and bloodlessness. It was obviously incipient consumption. In her own words: "Sharp cutting pains pierced through my lungs at every breath, and sometimes a fearful pain seized me round the heart. Eventually a hacking cough shook me and almost every night my bedclothes were soaked with the terrible night-sweats. At last, for 9 weary months I was too feeble to leave my bed, and I wasted away to a shadow." And yet Dr Williams Pink Pills cost only 2/9 a box.

False teeth were also extensively advertised. A full set of artificial teeth - "perfect for eating" - cost 20s from Shipley-Slipper, '"celebrated registered surgeon dentist"' in the High Street. A classified ad in the Tonbridge Free Press "Wanted - Old False Teeth" makes slightly disturbing reading.

There was little open discussion of mental illness. Some of the words used are a bit surprising. Lady Goldsmid left £1,000 to the Earlswood Asylum for Idiots. More surprising is a report of the Education Committee on proposals for the care of the feeble-minded. Mr Cripps, the Town Clerk, said that he thought that the 'lethal chamber' ie involuntary euthanasia, would be the best thing.

The Annual Report of the Medical Officer of Health includes statistics on employment from the Chief Sanitary Inspector. Taken together with the census they provide some interesting details. Of the 9,580 males of 14 and over in the 1901 census, 2,083 (22%) were retired or unoccupied. This might seem high, and we might assume that this was particular to Tunbridge Wells, but it was broadly the same in Southborough and Tonbridge. Of the active adult male population, 1,483 (20%) were involved in building, which would indicate why the town was so badly affected by a decline in the building industry; 1,121 (15%) were involved in 'Conveyance, of Men, Goods and

Messages', which includes railway workers and the Post Office; and 1,107 (15%) in the provision of 'Food, Tobacco, Drink and Lodgings'. Unfortunately 25% are classified as 'Other'. The only other significant numbers are in 'Agriculture - Farms, Woods and Gardens' which accounted for 486 (6%), and 'Dress' with 380 (5%). The MOH report gives us a few more detailed figures: 121 bakers, 53 blacksmiths, and 150 printers.

The female occupations are very different. Approximately two thirds are described as 'retired/unoccupied'. A large proportion of these 'unoccupied' women will have been married women looking after home and family. Of the others, 3,394 were domestic servants; 509 worked in laundries; 797 were dressmakers; 402 were involved with 'Food, Drink and Lodgings', and 232 were teachers.

It is disappointing that the figures do not identify the number who worked in shops. During August, members of the Council were pondering three work-related issues, and the first was to do with shops.

In July a petition was submitted by 27 out of the 33 hairdressers in the town requesting that the Council use its powers under the Shop Hours Act of 1904 to enforce early closing on Wednesdays for their trade. The council was not enthusiastic. Ald. Robb called it "tyranny of the worst form". Ald. Delves thought that England was becoming over-governed - mealtimes would be regulated next; and it would require the appointment of an inspector - at a cost to the rates. Yet other shops already had similar arrangements. The drapers had announced in December 1900 that they would operate such a scheme.

The early closing legislation was part of the movement to improve the lives of shopworkers. In the later years of the 19th century they typically worked from 7:30 or 8 in the morning until 8 or 9 o'clock in the evening, with extra late hours on Saturdays. Hours were eventually restricted in 1892, to a maximum of 72 a week. There was also a law of 1899, which required that shops should provide one seat for every three female workers. During 1909 the MOH visited 125 shops and reported no complaints about seats.

In many cases shop-workers 'lived in' - in dormitories over the premises. Weeke's, for example had 14 assistants living in - young women between 18 and 29. Sibthorpe's had six. Noake's in Calverley

RULES.—*Continued.*	FINES. s. d.	RULES (*Continued*).	FINES. s. d.
17. Reading Books or Newspapers, Gossiping or Loitering on the Premises, or making unnecessary noise, whether serving or not ..	1 0	23. Each Assistant to see own special orders are executed by the time promised, or letter of explanation sent to Customer	1 0
18. For omitting or taking a wrong address, or carelessly packing Customers' Parcels, or omitting to have the goods called back ..	1 0	24. Premiums to be shown on Bill and duplicate, and signed at same time as Bill ; amount to be given in to office each morning, with book added up, by 9.15	0 6
19. Standing on Cane-Bottomed or Show-Room Chairs, or giving wrong measure	0 6	25. Instructions for sending Parcels to be filed at once in office ; and none promised to special time without permission ..	0 6
20. Omitting to see that the Change is given out correctly at the office and also counted out correctly to Customers	1 0	26. Errors in entering or crediting goods or pattern books, or omitting to do so	1 0
21. Losing Sale of any Article without calling attention of the Principal, Foreman, or First Hand in the department to same ..	2 6	27. No discount to be allowed on Cottons, Calicoes, Gloves, or any goods charged nett price ..	1 0
22. Every Bill must have the department letter written in the margin to each line in consecutive order with date at heading. The Bill to be called back and signed before packing goods and amount received placed at bottom of left hand corner of Bill, and Customer to be informed of the amount so notified	1 0	28. All gas to be lighted with a taper. Using lighted paper or matches 29. Any duplicate short in book must be at once reported to office ; books to be checked when given out. Omission .. .. 30. These Rules to be returned to the office on Assistants leaving, or will be charged for ..	0 6 0 6 0 6

Rule Book for staff at Waymark's - Courtesy of Ruth Wakefield

Road had 14 young women and six young men under the care of a housekeeper and cook. The system was tied in with the idea of apprenticeship, and may have appealled to the parents of youngsters leaving home for the first time: a bed was provided, and meals, there was a curfew and supervision. But it could be a miserable sort of existance and demeaning for young adults, and the local Shop Assistants' Union certainly complained about it. HG Wells described it in both *Kipps* and *Mr Polly*. Particularly disliked was the system of fines, by which a petty discipline could be enforced.The rules typically covered both domestic arrangements, such as curfews, and work itself. Rule 3 at Waymarks (see above) stated "Assistants must do their very best to please Customers, and use the utmost civility to all". There was a penalty of 6d for trangressions. There was a higher fine of 1s, for allowing a customer to leave the Shop without being served (Rule 4). Selfridge's claimed that it could manage its staff without fines, and a lively debate ensued in the trade press.

Edmund Allen who managed the group of shops at the corner of Camden and Garden Roads (right) decided to allow his staff to 'sleep out'. He claimed it gave him so much more productive space**: a

**And they were able to sell the furniture at Brackett's, and raise £7. 3s.

private office for himself; a cashiers room with a network of pneumatic cash railways, and the latest National Cash Register. The assistants' dining room become a costume department; their kitchen provided splendid accommodation for mantles and ladies' outfitting; and even

the scullery could be used for stock. As for the staff, according to *Society*, "'Diana' of Edmund Allen's has a very good time of it indeed - she finishes her daily round by 8 o'clock and is then free to spend her time as she likes".

Another difference between Selfridge's and the typical British store, according to *The Times*, was "the pleasant habit of the shop assistants in refraining from asking what they could do for one". The British shop assistant may have specialised in an obsequious politeness, but their clear objective was to sell.**

** For an excellent thumbnail sketch of a draper's assistant in action, see the first page of HG Wells *The Wheels of Chance*.

The second 'labour' issue facing the Council related to the town's police force. In August the Rev DJ Stather Hunt presented a petition urging the Council to allow them two days off each month. At the time they only had one day a month (plus seven days annual leave). Cllr Edwards objected, saying that the police only worked from 6am to 2pm, and then had the rest of the day free, but eventually it was accepted. The Met Police apparently, had a day off every week.

And finally, there was the question of the Wednesday evening postal delivery. A new postmaster proposed to the Council that the 7pm delivery be suspended; it was, after all, early closing day. There was a mixed response. Cllr Carpenter thought it excellent that the postmen should have one evening a week when they could work in their garden. Cllr Emson disagreed, citing the inconvenience to professional men - a letter sent to London in the morning, would no longer get a reply the same day. A wider consultation was conducted through the letters page of the *Courier*. One letter said that it would cause great hardship to businessmen, who would move to other towns. Did the councillors want more empty houses in the town? Cllr Badcock, in contrast, thought it a most reasonable request. Eastbourne and Hastings only had five deliveries a day - why did Tunbridge Wells need six? It would be a great boon to a hard-working body of men. A letter the following week denied that they were hard-working. They were well paid, received good Christmas boxes, and a pension on retiring. The proposal was rejected by the Council.

*   *   *

The big events of the summer - Cricket Week, the Agricultural Show - were in July, but the 'season' continued through the summer. It is difficult to get accurate figure for the number of visitors. One method is to count the number of names printed in the *Gazette* each week of those staying in boarding houses and apartments. Clearly it is an imperfect - only those volunteering their names were included, and hotel guests were excluded, so the figures must be a significant under-estimate. Nevertheless they give us something to work with, and show very little seasonal variation.

March 17th	277
May 19th	344
July 21st	329
Sept 15th	402

** The fact that visitors brought their own maids and nurses is frequently mentioned In fact the numbers were small. The list for June 2nd, for example, included only 4 nurses and 6 maids.

The figures include maids, and nurses**. The proportion of females varies from 76% to 81%. Even more than the residents, the visitors to Tunbridge Wells were overwhelmingly female. The advantage of males is that we can make some assumptions about background from their title. Of the 297 who are listed, 22 (8%) had a military or naval rank, 22 had a clerical title, and 11 were doctors.

So what did the visitors do? At a Tradesmen's Association meeting in June, Mr HJ Wilmott, criticising the Council's meagre allowance for the Band, said: "Afternoon meetings, magic lanterns by night, and meditative walks on the Pantiles are pastimes too mild to give general satisfaction." And yet they seemed to satisfy the visitors.

- They went to the Pantiles and listened to the Band.
- They went to the Great Hall and Opera House in the afternoons and evenings** for concerts or talks.
- They went on outings - to High Rocks, Happy Valley and Toad Rock. You could go to High Rocks by wagonnette for 6d, or hire a landau with coachman and pair for 10/6 an hour.
- They took out temporary membership of the Tunbridge Wells Club, and of Williams' Library.
- They compared the preaching skills of the different clergy.

Lewis Melville contrasted the visiters in 1911 with those in earlier centuries: "Folks in all ranks of life ... go there today; but it is for seclusion, not for gaiety; to avoid the Fashion, not to meet it." Many visitors came for the walking. One of them described arriving after a 30-mile hike: from Woking to Guildford and then Redhill to Tunbridge Wells. Another wrote of walking 10 to 12 miles a day "traversing the transcendently beautiful walks which abound around the town." This writer was not impressed by the town's postal service - he objected to being woken at 7am "a well-nigh nocturnal visitation".

We can read their views from the back of their post-cards. One went to the Congregational Church twice and enjoyed the service very much. Another sent a picture of Holy Trinity with the message "This is the church we go to. The Vicar, Mr Stather Hunt preaches so well." They were quite prepared to try different churches. One Welsh visitor, writing to the *Courier* said that there had been 1,200 at a service in Holy Trinity, but that he had also enjoyed Emmanuel. He also praised the fly-drivers, saying there was no vulgar language.

** Afternoon performances were usually more expensive - I suspect that they catered for a more select audience of visitors, and those 'living on their own means'

Picture post-cards were introduced in the 1890's. Their attraction was that they were cheap and fast. They even record the changing weather on a particular day. We have a card (a picture of the Common) sent at 11:30 on Sept 7th, from 'May' at the Hunters Hotel in the High Street. She reports their arrival in the town, and that "the air is so strong and lovely", though the train upset Sylvie a little. At 6:45 that evening Sylvie herself sent a card (of Happy Valley) saying that they got caught in a thunderstorm during the afternoon - so much for the lovely strong air.

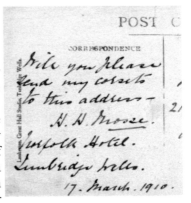

You could also use a post-card to ask your family to send on things that you had forgotten (see right), though one does wonder how she(?) managed to leave home without her corset. Or maybe the Norfolk Hotel was more straight-laced than she had expected. As with all new things, there were complaints about post-cards. They were blamed for 'the curt brevity of modern correspondence". It was a consequence of the "rush and whirl in which we live. There is no time for letter writing in these busy scrambling days."

Other Events in August

Jenkin Lloyd again

Evan Jenkin Lloyd, who attacked his wife back in February, was in trouble again in early August - accused of drunkenness and of bursting into the offices of Vaughan Gower, his wife's solicitor. A separation order was granted to Mrs Lloyd. Two days later he was found unconscious. He had taken 72 grains of Veronal, a sleeping drug. In the flat were two letters to his wife which had been returned unopened. In them he had pleaded with her to take him back, and had threatened to kill himself. He was charged with attempted suicide. When the case came up at the Quarter Sessions in October, he vehemently denied the charge, and was found not guilty.

September

Typical Anti-Budget League cartoon - Lloyd George, in
trying to attack Capital, is harming the working man

In which we consider:

- **The Continuing Debate over Lloyd George's Budget**
- **Education in Tunbridge Wells**
- **Local Omnibus Services**
- **Entertainment**

It is quite normal for a Budget to generate excitement and comment at the time that it is announced, but that excitement usually dies away. This didn't happen in 1909 - the intensity of the argument increased. Opposition by the House of Lords, especially to the proposed tax on the unearned increase in the value of land, led to a constitutional crisis - should the Lords be allowed to vote down a budget passed by the elected House of Commons? There were those who said that Lloyd George deliberately engineered the conflict with the Lords. His Limehouse speech on 30th July on the theme 'their day of reckoning is at hand' was one of his most powerful.

Residents of Tunbridge Wells could not escape the argument. The *Courier* moved its campaigning away from Tariff Reform to concentrate on opposition to the Budget. Week after week it published cartoons of Lloyd George, characterised as a Socialist, attacking the British economy and constitution. The *Advertiser*, normally more restrained, presented the pro-budget message. Budget campaigning dominated some of the traditional summer events: the Primrose League Fete at Eridge Castle in early August, and the Unionist Fete at Somerhill the following week. In early September the anti- and pro- Budget factions both held demonstrations in Tunbridge Wells. Reporting of the events in the two papers was noticeably partisan.

There was no suggestion of crowd trouble at either demonstration, though this was evident elsewhere. The *Courier* reported on a speech in Tonbridge by an anti-Budget spokesman from Lancashire There was constant and unpleasant heckling: "the opprobrious epithets and the foul and disgusting language ... must have been abhorrent and nauseous to all self-respecting people". The Chairman made the mistake of calling the interrupter a 'cad'. The hecklers booed and hissed and tried to pull him off the waggon.The interrupters now had a grievance, and called for an apology, or they would turn the waggon over. The Chairman refused, and the meeting ended in uproar. The speaker claimed that in all his experience in Lancashire he had never heard such filthy and disgusting language.

The Mayor was brought into the argument. He described the Budget as "an honest attempt to fit the burden to the back most capable of bearing it", but said that he was too occupied to have studied it. The *Courier* was scornful of someone who proffered an opinion on something and yet was too busy to study it.

*   *   *

A letter in the *Courier* of 27th August pointed out that school children in London were back at school after a month, and asked why Tunbridge Wells children of a similar class were allowed to roam streets and roads for six weeks. At least the writer recognised that there were some benefits in compulsory education for all, if only to keep the streets clear.

Most children went to church schools. Many of these survive today, though not always on the same site. The children attended from age five to fourteen. The main, Church of England, schools, with their average numbers are listed below. The figures in brackets show the percentage of pupils who were provided with boots from the Boot Fund in 1908. Schools without a percentage figure may have operated their own internal scheme.

- Christ Church (which was on the site of the 'Safeway' supermarket - see over page): 47 infants, 86 seniors (12%)
- Holy Trinity Infants (between Basinghall Lane and Goods Station Road): 231 (5%)
- Holy Trinity Girls (York Road): 216.
- Holy Trinity Boys (Royal Victoria School) (Calverley St): 229 (2%)
- King Charles' Boys (behind King Charles Church): 256.
- St Barnabas: 145 infants, 109 girls, 143 boys (15%)
- St James' (in Quarry Road, opposite St Barnabas): 299 infants, 228 girls, 262 boys
- St John's (on the corner of Newcomen Road): 190 seniors (27%)
- Down Lane Infants: 240 (25%)
- St Luke's Infants: 155 (30%)
- St Mark's (in Frant Road, near corner of Birling Road): 90 infants, 140 seniors
- St Peter's: 99 infants, 108 girls, 138 boys (8%)

The King Charles Girls and Infants School, usually called Murray House, is probably missing from the list because it was being re-built in 1909. The new building was opened in November.

There was also: St Augustine's School, for Catholics, in Hanover Road, with 97 pupils (27%); the Grosvenor United school (on the site of the Meadow Road car-park) for non-conformists, with 150 (1%); and a 'mission school' in Varney St with 68 (29%).

Middle class children went to small private schools, or were educated at home. Joan Burslem went first to a small school in Calverley Road: "I went to Miss Lines' at the age of four and a half, and learned

Christ Church School - oppostie the South-Eastern station.

there to read and write and do simple sums. There was no question of 'educative play' in those days. At five and a half I went to the Misses Barnes' school at 69 The Pantiles. I walked there and back with an older girl - she was ten - there was no question of it not being safe to do so. There we were taught a limited range of subjects extremely well. We also had dancing lessons. Miss Julia sat by and beat our feet with a small cane when we went wrong."

The principal private schools for girls were Hamilton House in Amherst Road and Miss Vickery's in Frant Road. These were strictly for 'ladies' - the children of tradesmen were not admitted. The education was fairly limited - the 3 R's needlework, dancing, manners, etc. A small school for girls, Newton House, in Woodbury Park Road admitted all classes. Here the education was similarly limited, but more emphasis was placed on religious teaching.

Education had been compulsory since 1870, but there were still those who questioned its value for the lower classes. Lady Dorothy Nevill blamed it for the increase in strikes: " it merely teaches children enough to be discontented with the lowly station in life in which, perforce, a great majority of the world must remain." ** She was particularly concerned that good manners were not being taught: "Formerly when a child was brought into contact with any older person, it was but natural for it to behave with a respectful politeness ... little girls, for instance ... gave a graceful curtsey when they passed any grown-up ... and little boys touched their caps, old-fashioned ways, which, to a great extent, have now been superseded by a sort of "I'm as good as you" kind of air."

** Lady Dorothy was 83 in 1909. Neither did she approve of free libraries.

110

Yet this was not the memory of those who attended the town schools. Harvey Dunn was at King Charles in 1905: "We had to raise our caps to all, not just to touch them, and address Teachers and Elders as 'Sir'." They also had to show the teacher their handkerchief each morning, after registration: "I will not tolerate my boys wiping their noses on their sleeves."

According to Mr Dunn, they were taught the 3 R's, and each afternoon had handwriting lessons with copy books. Arithmetic and Grammar were always part of the homework. He felt that they were being trained for clerical jobs at the Town Hall. If so, they were being set far loftier targets than most girl pupils. Cllr Wesley Smith, at a prize-giving at St Peters Girls' School, said that he laid great stress on cooking and needlework, for they must remember that later on they would be the housewives of the land, and they should be able to carry out their duties with competency.

The links between schools and churches meant that there was usually some wealthy supporter who could provide a field or large garden for a summer 'treat' . The children of St Peter's School were due to go to 'Ravensdale' in Pembury Road - but the ground was not ready, so the treat was held in the Parish Rooms instead. The children enjoyed jam sandwiches, buns and Bohea (a cheap form of tea). They had games and a gramophone. St Mark's went to Moat Farm; St James' to Sherwood; St Barnabas to Charity Farm; and Emmanuel by train to Frant, where they joined their counterparts from Bells Yew Green. The luckiest seem to have been those from King Charles who went to Hastings for the day.

In May the Head Teachers' Association held a conference. The guest speaker emphasised the importance of sleep. It was said that one of the failings of children in Tunbridge Wells was that they didn't get to bed on time. The upper classes were just as bad as the others - taking their children to the theatre in the evening. Mr Wheatley (St John's) blamed it on homework - the children talked about it in their sleep. The January edition of *Girls Own Paper and Women's Magazine* felt the same way - criticising the urge to over-educate young children at an age when the brain couldn't stand the strain.

Most of those leaving the elementary schools at fourteen would become apprentices, or, if they were girls, go into service, or become 'the daughter at home'. For some there was the possibility of going on to secondary school. The two secondary schools for boys - the

Skinners' School in Tunbridge Wells and the Judd Commercial School in Tonbridge had opened in 1887 and 1888. They were fee-paying, but with the possibility of scholarships and exhibitions. Skinners, which described itself as offering "a good, modern and commercial education, such as fits boys for a useful career in business", charged annual fees of £11.5s (£8.5s for under elevens). It had 165 pupils in 1909, 22 of them were boarders.

There was also the County School for Girls. This was formed in 1905 at the Technical Institute, at least partly to train pupil teachers. It then merged with an existing private school at Vale Towers, and stayed there until 1911. It then moved to Southfield Road, and evolved, eventually, into TWGGS. In 1909 it had 149 pupils, aged between 8 and 18. 105 were fee-paying (£9.3s for the over twelves), 29 had county scholarships or bursaries, and 15 were student or pupil teachers. The girls learned maths and classics, history, geography, nature, needlework, scripture and singing. And elocution - one girl remembered that they "set about eliminating our Kentish vowels with great determination".

Once a week they had gymnastics at the Pump Room, though preparation took up a lot of the time: "so much outdoor clothing had to be donned and doffed and donned again; laced and buttoned boots, the hard straw 'boater' school hat, and of course gloves - no lady, we were adjured, ever went out, winter or summer, without her gloves." There were six mistresses, all unmarried. Their annual salary was about £113, an equivalent male teacher received £140 to £160.

We can compare the family backgrounds of the girls against those in similar schools in Tonbridge and the rest of Kent:

	T Wells	Tonb	Kent
Indep/Prof	21.9	18.55	26.6
Retail Traders	45.26	30.93	27.4
Clerks, etc	12.41	8.24	19.2
Farmers	15.32	14.43	6.1
Artisans	5.11	27.83	20.7

The relatively low Tunbridge Wells figure for Independent/Professional families may be because these families favoured the alternative Girls' High School in Cambridge Gardens. This saw itself as occupying "for Girls the position taken in the education of Boys by the great public Schools". In 1909 it was attempting to introduce uniform. The girls were opposed - a uniform might suggest that they were charity children. An ex-pupil who started as a nine year-old in 1903 spoke of the "awe-inspiring aspect of the prefects with hair up and skirts to their ankles. These august beings were far more remote than the mistresses".

The school tried to introduce gymnastics, though again there was opposition. Many parents objected, saying that the girls were becoming too immodest in their short black tunics and blue blouses. An annual gym display was started, but the audience was restricted to mothers and those fathers who were doctors. The girls themselves hardly helped. The gym teacher wrote: "It was very nice to see so many tunics in the Tuesday drill classes, and if only the corset trouble could be got over, I am sure that better work would be done. What is the use of putting a nice loose tunic over a pair of corsets?"

Since 1902 all elementary schools had been supported out of the rates. In Tunbridge Wells most of them were Church of England schools, and one was Catholic. This upset some non-conformists, who felt that they were being forced to pay for teaching that was contrary to their beliefs. A campaign of 'passive resistance' developed. In February, and August each year,a group of 30 or so were brought to court for failure to pay their Rates in full. It was very embarassing for the authorities, many of whom were themselves non-conformist. Bailiffs seized the property of the resisters, and the items were put up for auction in the Town Hall. The only people present were the auctioneers, the police and the resisters, who bought back their goods at previously agreed prices. It was all very orderly, everyone doing their jobs, and keen to make it clear that there was no personal animosity.

*   *   *

An article in the June 6th *Advertiser* tells the story of a supposed Bank Holiday visit to the Wells by three young friends. They like the waters, but not enough to have a second glass; they admire the Opera House - quite different from places of amusement in 'common' towns; and they like the shops of Mount Pleasant, but one of them is puzzled by the lack of trams. He is corrected by his friend - buses are far more appropriate, trams just would not accord with the dignity of a royal borough. It is a social distinction that I had not previously encountered, but it was obviously important. In January, the *Advertiser* reported that the tramways in Maidstone had lost £700 in six months, and called them an "abomination" that would never do in Tunbridge Wells.

There had been omnibuses serving Tunbridge Wells since the 1860's. In 1909 they were operated by the Tunbridge Wells, Southborough and District Omnibus Co. The main service ran half-hourly between the Brighton station and the 'Hand & Sceptre' in Southborough, though there were also services to Pembury, Langton and Speldhurst, Hawkenbury, and along Upper Grosvenor Road.

The company held its AGM in June, reporting a loss of £24.11.4 which it blamed on the bad weather. It had introduced new buses in March - in white enamel, picked out with vermillion, and with bright yellow seats and wheels. It also introduced new, friskier, horses. A lady traveller wrote to the *Advertiser* saying how much she enjoyed the ride between Waymark's corner and Queens Road. Despite the cold and the snow, she had imagined herself driving her own team.

In April, the *Advertiser*'s etiquette expert, Mrs Humphry ('Madge' of *Truth*), advised on the correct behaviour when using an omnibus. When escorting a lady, a gentleman hands her into the omnibus before entering himself. If she prefers the top, he lets her mount in front of him. Mrs Humphry was keen to correct the idea that one should precede a lady up and down the stairs - that was "not in accordance with the practice of good society". And it was by no means necessary that a man should resign his seat in or on an omnibus simply because a woman wished for it. The conductor had no right to ask "if any gentleman will go outside to oblige a lady", and no gentlewoman would allow him to ask such a favour on her behalf.

In June the Omnibus Company was forced to prosecute nine of its staff for fraud. There seems to have been two schemes operating. In one, a roll of tickets was stolen fom the office, and used by the conductors who then kept the fares. In the other, the conductors re-used tickets picked up from the floor. Mr Vaughan Gower, prosecuting, suggested that the conductors (aged 16 and 17) had been led astray by the drivers. Questioned by the Bench, the conductors explained that they were paid 6/6 to 7/- a week, for working 12 hours a day. Mr Gower pointed out that they also received tips. They were bound over to keep the peace for twelve months. The drivers, who earned between 18/- and £1 a week, were fined £5, or a month in gaol. The following week Ephraim Draper, 59, of Southborough, one of the drivers was found drowned in the fish pond of Great Bounds Park. His brothers had offered to help him find the money to avoid going to gaol, but he had not been in good health, and did not expect to find other work.

A bigger threat to the omnibus company arose in August. The Council received an application from the Autocar Company to run motor buses between Southborough and the Brighton station. It was not certain that the Council would approve the application. In June they had rejected a proposal from the Sutton Valence Steam Bus Co for a

route from Sutton Valence. The *Advertiser* was concerned - the existing company might be driven out of business by a service that might prove in the long run to be less reliable. But the Council did approve the

**These were not the first motor buses in the town. The TWS&DO Co had itself tried them in 1905, but they had not been a success. They were sold to Brighton, and one is apparently preserved in the USA.

application, on condition that the new buses passed strict tests. The bus company conducted a very effective PR campaign, feeding *Courier* reporters technical details and taking them for rides. The buses were said to have very powerful brakes, and especially powerful engines allowing them to climb hills practically noiselessly. They were the same width top and bottom, which avoided swaying. They were very smart machines, in polished ash and mahogany. Even the drivers looked different - in tweeds and caps, rather than the heavy overcoats and bowler hats favoured by horse bus drivers.

The motor buses proved to be a success. In August 1910 the horse bus company went into liquidation. In September a new horse bus service was started, but this only lasted until 1912. Some horse buses remained, to serve the outlying villages, but effectively the motor bus had won.

*   *   *

Back in 1902 they had called it the Opera House rather than a Theatre because "many of the good people of Tunbridge Wells looked askance at any sort of theatrical performance". But times had changed, and in 1909 the good people flocked to watch a dancer who was said to perform wearing only two oyster shells and a five-franc piece.

Maud Allen was not a classically trained dancer. Rather she 'interpreted' the music in her own unique way. The *Courier* described it as "undulating". She had shocked London with her portrayal of Salome and had been banned by the Watch Committee in Manchester; but a private performance for the King at Marienbad had given her a 'must-see' credibility. Sir Frederick Ponsonby, the King's Private Secretary, described her dance as "really wonderful ... although I cannot say she wore many clothes, there was nothing the least indecent about her performance". She came to Tunbridge Wells on September 10th and was welcomed by a large and fashionable audience. In the words of the *Courier*, "the motions of the slight

but perfect figure exercised a peculiar fascination over the observers".

The Opera House and Great Hall competed to present a wide range of theatrical events. The Great Hall tended towards more serious music. In January it presented the violinist Fritz Kreisler. According to *Society*, "A very large audience went to worship at the shrine of genius ... no-one can approach him for the liquid sweetness of his tone power ... he has no equal in interpretive ability". But the Great Hall could also advertise: 'Miss Frederica's Wonderful Performing Terriers and 'Dot' the Cake-Walking Pony'; and in December hosted Fred Karno's music-hall.

The Opera House tended more to drama. We have already mentioned *An Englishman's Home* in April. There was a Shakespearean season in May - seven plays in six days. A production of *The Passing of the Third Floor Back* on August Bank Holiday had a big impact. These days, the play, by Jerome K Jerome, is said to be too sentimental to be staged, but to *Society* it was "A beautiful play. A play to revive one's faith in human nature. A play to make you think." And the *Advertiser* described it as a play in which is blended "the genius of the novelist, the perfected art of the playwright, and the powerful magnetism of the great preacher". How sad that we are too sophisticated to appreciate it.

Clara Butt, the contralto, made her annual visit in November, with her husband Kennerley Rumford. Their programme contained a new piece based on the work of Hilaire Belloc, including the story of Matilda, who told lies and was burned to death. By popular request she also sang *Abide with Me*. In November also, the pianist Paderewski appeared. He gave a performance of "exquisite taste and delicacy", though in great pain from neuralgia.The Opera House also specialised in music hall, with seasons dedicated to the 'Hippodrome Theatre of Varieties'.

Once a year, and for one day only, the circus came to town. The *Advertiser* considered the circus procession on September 7th to have been the best for many years, and the two performances in the huge tent on the Common excellent. The show included the driving of a "fully-laden 40 hp Argyll motor-car" over the body of CYCLO - the human enigma with loins of steel.

Other Events in September

ONLY 14 WEEKS TO CHRISTMAS - BUY YOUR PIANO NOW (advert in *Courier* 17th September)

First Man to reach the North Pole

On September 1st 1909 (New York time) it was announced that the American explorer, Dr Frederick Albert Cook had reached the North Pole on April 21st 1908.His return had been delayed by bad weather. On September 6th 1909 (New York time) it was announced that the American explorer, Cmdr Robert E Peary had reached the North Pole on April 6th 1909. The dispute as to which, if either, of them actually got there first, went on for some time, and, to some extent, still goes on. Peary is generally accorded the honour.

The Missing Five Pound Notes

When one could live a comfortable middle-class life on £600 a year and many working people earned less than £2.10s a week, most financial transactions were done in shillings and pennies (and silver threepenny bits). For larger amounts there were pound coins - sovereigns - made of gold, but no pound or ten-shilling notes. There were £5 notes but they were so unusual that on receipt their serial numbers were often recorded. Which could be useful.

In February, Lucy Collins withdrew £80 in £5 notes from the Post Office. In April five of the notes were stolen. Using the serial numbers recorded by the Post Office, the police were able to identify all the ones that she and her sister had spent in St Johns Road and Mount Ephraim. Five notes which were identified in Tenterden were therefore the stolen ones. Tracking these notes via a bank, a baker and a dealer led the police to William Swift. He claimed that he had found them in a pair of second-hand trousers bought in Ashford.The police must have been very pleased with their detective work, Swift even admitted to being in Tonbridge in April. But a jury wasn't convinced and he was found not-guilty at the County Court in October.

October

Male Inmates at the Tonbridge Workhouse. c 1897.
(c) Peter Higginbotham / www.workhouses.org.uk

In which we consider:

- **Begging and Slate Clubs**

- **The Workhouse**

- **Hops**

- **Food**

- **Plans for a new Skating Rink**

One of the more noticeable things about 1909 was the amount of begging though it is perhaps mainly noticeable because reports of begging are one of the first things that one reads in the *Courier*.

Most of the beggars were harmless characters, and received minor punishments: JW Wilson, begging in Mount Ephraim Road, said he had a situation to go to, and was fined 1s. Some of them were aggressive: Thomas Payne, an unlicensed peddlar of picture postcards arrested in Frant Road, was unlicensed specifically because he became abusive when his goods were refused. He was fined 10s or 14 days in prison. Some were con-men, such as well-dressed William Pope who followed a commuter up from the station to Molyneux Park, and persuaded him to spare the fare to St Leonards. He tried the same trick a few days later, and was unfortunate enough to pick on the wife of his first victim. He got 14 days. The worst example was Herbert Smith, aka John Wilson, who came to Tunbridge Wells by train one morning, and claimed to be collecting money for the family of a railway guard killed in an accident. He got to the house of Mr E Symes JP who called the police. He was brought to court, sentenced to two months and sent off to Maidstone that same day.

In January the magistrates said that they were determined to put down the begging nuisance and sentenced Frank Ratcliffe to 14 days hard labour for begging in Chapel Place. But that strategy did not work. The same phrase - being determined to put down begging - was used again in June when Ann Kemsley used her children when begging in Culverden Park. Once somebody got into the situation of needing to beg, it was difficult to climb out.

There were steps that could be taken to avoid it, like contributing to a Friendly Society - these offered support at times of sickness and old age, in return for small regular sums - 4d perhaps or 6d. One of them, the Manchester Unity of Oddfellows had over a million members. In Tunbridge Wells they were based in the Friendly Societies' Hall in Camden Road**. There were also 'slate clubs', much smaller affairs but based on the same mutual principles. The difference was that any surplus at the end of the year was distributed, providing a handy bonus at Christmas. The Albion Road Sick Benefit Society, for example, had 130 members. During 1908 it had collected £193 in subscripions. It had disbursed £60 in sickness and widows' benefits. Members therefore received a bonus of 19/6 each.

** This housed some 25 building societies, friendly societies, and similar.

And then there was the workhouse, just outside Pembury on the road to Tonbridge - far enough away to be out of sight, but very much in mind for the aged poor, and those in financial difficulties.

Workhouses were established by the Poor Law Amendment Act of 1834. This ended centuries-old arrangements by which the poor were supported in their home parishes. The 1834 Act brought in two changes: it forced most of those seeking relief to go into the workhouse to get it; and it required parishes to combine into 'Unions', and centralise their facilities. The workhouse in Pembury belonged to the Tonbridge Union,which comprised Tonbridge, Tunbridge Wells and ten rural parishes from Ashurst to Hadlow and Brenchley. The workhouse itself was built in 1836 with major extensions in the 1890's. In 1909 it housed some four to five hundred inmates, their numbers peaking in the winter months; plus an average of forty to fifty 'casuals' - their numbers peaking in the summer months.

The workhouse master was William Gane. He had a staff of about thirty, two-thirds of whom were nurses in the infirmary. These were supplemented by inmates acting as 'helpers'. Other officers worked outside: the Relieving Offices in the parishes, who determined which cases were eligible for entry; and the Collection Officers, who brought in the funds, both by the application of the Poor Rate, and by seeking contributions from the family members of those inside. Despite its notorious penny-pinching, the workhouse was an expensive operation**, and the Poor Rate didn't just hit the wealthy. In *The Ragged Trousered Philanthropists***** in the scene when the young house-painter and his wife are reviewing the bills that they must pay from the £1/4/9 that he has finally managed to earn, a final demand for Poor Rate of £1/1/5 is particularly hard to meet.

The workhouse was managed by a board of elected Guardians. Three of them were women, one of whom, Amelia Scott, later wrote her memoirs in *The Passing of a Great Dread*. The introduction of women Guardians in significant numbers in the 1890's led to improved conditions for the inmates****.

** The annual sum charged to the Poor Rate may have been c £50,000

*** I know it's just a story, but it's a story written in the years around 1909, and in a town, Hastings, not so very far from Tunbridge Wells.

****One of the earlier campaigners for improvements was Louisa Twining (1820-1912). She lived in Tunbridge Wells (St James' Road) in the 1890's and served as a Guardian for four years.

Tonbridge Workhouse early 1900's
(c) Peter Higginbotham / www.workhouses.org.uk

People ended up in the workhouse for many reasons, but they fall perhaps into three groups: the aged, the infirm and the destitute. Vera Coomber has studied the number of elderly (60+) admissions during this period. In 1909 there were 290 - about 30% of the total. We might compare that with the number of the people aged 60+ in the Tonbridge Union as a whole, which was c 7,000. So the proportion who ended their days in the workhouse was fairly small. The Receiving Officers were allowed to grant 'outdoor relief' to older people in the community. In November over 1,200 people benefitted (661 in Tunbridge Wells), though the sums were small, as low as 2/- a week**. Vera's figures suggest that the majority of those aged 60+ who entered the house were single men - widowers mainly.

To go into the house at that age was a major step, there was rarely any possibility of returning to normal life. You gave up your own clothes for a workhouse uniform, stamped with the words 'Tonbridge Union'; you slept in a dormitory; you gave up all personal possessions save those that would fit in a small locker. By 1909 there had been improvements. Those aged inmates considered to be respectable were allowed little privileges: to leave the house for a half-day every month; to receive rations of tea and tobacco (in the Master's Day Book of expenses there was a heading of 'Necessaries'. This included expenditure on soap, coal and gas; but also tobacco - an order worth £3.10s each month). But as with all inmates the elderly were subject

** Despite the small amounts involved there were complaints in 1908 that being in receipt of outdoor relief had disqualified some of those aged 70+ from receiving Old Age Pensions.

to the petty tyrannies of the officials. Amelia Scott remembers a new Charge Nurse who cleared the lockers of the Women's Infirm Ward, of the small mementoes that were all that was left of their previous lives.

There was nothing actually stopping the other inmates from discharging themselves whenever they wanted. There developed the concept of the 'in and outs' - mainly families of agricultural labourers who entered the house for the winter and left again in the spring when work was available. This disrupted the education of the children. One particular family from Capel practised this in-and-out behaviour to the extreme: admitted on 9th Dec 1908; discharged on 2nd January; re-admitted on 5th Jan; discharged on 9th Feb; in again on 13th Feb; and out on the 15th; in on 13th March and out on 6th April; in on the 14th and out again on the 20th.

It was not a pleasant life for the children. Miss Scott describes the Nursery - for those up to three years old. It was on the third-floor, and had no furniture, no toys and no carpets. The children were just left on the floor all day. They never went outside. And there is a memory from the Tenterden workhouse of how normal routines were often strangely distorted. On her birthday a young girl was thrilled to receive a doll from the matron. She played with it all day. In the evening the matron told her that she should put it away carefully in a cupboard, to keep it clean. She never saw it again, and later learned that the same doll was presented to every little girl on her birthday.

Female Inmates at the Tonbridge Workhouse.
c 1897.
(c) Peter Higginbotham / www.workhouses.org.uk

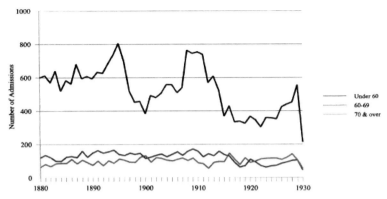

Admissions to the Tonbridge Workhouse 1880-1930. Vera Coomber 1996

For a while the workhouse educated the children in-house, but by 1909 they were being sent to school in Pembury. This at least gave them some exposure to the outside world, but it also exposed them to the cruelties of that world. With their workhouse uniforms and workhouse haircuts they were an easy target for abuse from the other children.

There was a large increase in the number of admissions in 1909 due to the economic situation, and a corresponding increase in the number of children (up from c.45 to c.75). Concern was expressed by the school, and by the Local Government Board inspector. The workhouse sought to board out the children, offering 4s a week, but with little success. The Chairman of the Board rejected as extravagant a suggestion by the Inspector that they establish cottage homes for the children away from the main house**.

About a third of the inmates were in the infirmary, suffering either the chronic ailments of the old, or diseases like TB and cancer. There was a staff of trained and probationer nurses, but no resident doctor and very limited facilities. The Medical Officer, though, was concerned about standards, and complained to the Master in November about the practice of probationer nurses bathing male patients, some of them strong young men, and "many from the lowest classes of society". He felt it improper. The Master arranged for the bathing to be done by a male inmate.

** In fact within 4 or 5 years this had become the standard practice. A regulation of 1913 said that no child over 3 was to be kept in the same place as adults (partly to avoid malign influences, such as the young women who entered the workhouse for the birth of illegitimate children).

Then there were the casuals, who stayed only a night or two - who were only allowed to stay a night or two. The number averaged about 45 a night, through the autumn and winter. It went up to about 60 during the early summer, with a sudden peak at more than 140 for the last two weeks of August - presumably the effect of the hop-picking season. 80% were men, though there were women and children too. Some of the more colourful accounts of workhouse life are by social commentators who went on the tramp and experienced life as casuals. One of the worst aspects was the requirement to have a bath on entry - in bathwater that had already been used by dozens of other, not very clean individuals. At Pembury, the casual ward had no beds - hammocks were strung up in the evening. It had no chairs either, so they had to sit on the floor. The food was bread and cheese, with skilly - a form of gruel - served from a pail. The food given to the regular inmates was a little better but still consisted mainly of bread and porridge, and yet a new Cook appointed in November was sacked after a week "he has shown that he is quite incompetent to discharge his duties". I am not sure what to make of a complaint in April, that the patients in the infirmary were given Grape Nuts instead of porridge for breakfast. Casuals were required to work, typically at tasks like picking oakum or stone breaking. There were special cells at Pembury for this latter task. The work meant that they were not able to leave until half-way through the following day, and in a dirty and dishevelled state. There was an incident in May at Bromley workhouse where one of the casuals tried to shoot the Labour-Master "he is a dirty dog. I would murder him if I got him outside". It was not explained how the casual had managed to get a gun into the workhouse - they were supposed to be searched on entry.

*   *   *

The hop industry was very important to the area around Tunbridge Wells, and in 1909 it was in crisis. The main complaint was competition from abroad, specifically America (some of the best hops, it seems, were picked by Indians in Sacramento). The Liberal government, true to its Free Trade principles, and despite a huge demonstration in Trafalgar Square in 1908, refused to apply import duties to protect British producers.

The fight against Free Trade was the *Courier's* main campaign in the early months of 1909. The subject caused considerable embarassment to Paget Hedges, the MP. He tried to explain to hop-growers in Capel in January that the problem was not imports, but a reduction in the use of hops in beer-production, but his audience was not convinced and he was jostled on his way to his car. It was particularly embarassing because his own business, tobacco manufacture, was protected by duties. The issue was kept alive through the spring and summer by Viscount Hardinge of Penshurst who tried to introduce a Bill to ban artificial hop-substitutues and preservatives in beer (and thus increase the use of actual hops). In October came reports that the hop harvest was the worst since 1882. The weather had been awful, and there had been an infestation of aphis. The news for individual growers was bad, but for the industry as a whole it was good. The reduced supply, which affected overseas producers as well, meant that surplus stocks from previous years were quickly used up, and prices rose.

This was good news too for Tunbridge Wells Council - which produced hops near the South Farm sewage works. It sold the 1909 crop for £825. The production of bullocks on the North Farm also did well, raising £750. The North Farm was particularly suitable for this: stock could be released onto the grass only two days after sewage had been spread on it. Cllr Symes was teased by other councillors: "what about the loganberries?". He refused to be drawn. Unfortunately, the archives do not tell us what happened to them.

*   *   *

One of the achievements of the late Victorian period was an improvement in the purity of foodstuffs, resulting from various Food and Drugs Acts and the activities of public analysts. The quarterly results from the County Analyst for Kent were regularly reported in the *Courier*. A particular concern was the watering of milk. In May, 14% of 252 samples were affected. The analyst felt that they were "making headway against dishonest milkmen, though they are very stubborn people". He was also concerned about butter. Eight of 127 samples of butter in August contained more than 95% 'foreign fat', in other words they were margarine. 25% of the cocoa samples were adulterated, and 10% of the whisky. There were no mandatory standards for beer, other than it should not be 'injurious', but the Analyst was concerned about the possible addition of salt, to stimulate thirst.

The Borough Sanitary Inspector also played a role in food standards. His report for 1909 records that 47lb of kidney, 11lb of liver and 36lb of beef, had been taken before the magistrate, condemned and cremated in the furnace of the swimming baths. The report provides other items of interest, for example:

- nuisances - the Inspector tried to encourage cottagers to give up foul and offensive chicken runs in their back yards, and to grow flowers instead - these produced ozone which purified the air

- rubbish collection - the regulation time for the removal of rubbish was once every 9 days in winter, and once every 7 days in summer, though the council aimed to collect it once every 5 days during the hottest periods. The Inspector considered that the method of disposal - into the pit at the High Brooms Brick Works - was by no means satisfactory.

- disinfection - in 1909 the Inspector organised the disinfection of 575 rooms and 13,965 items of clothing. The requirement to disinfect a room and bedding after a death led to a court case in January where a Tunbridge Wells landlady successfully sued the relatives of a visitor who died of consumption 4 days after arrival. She insisted that they must have known of the woman's condition.

Lady Dorothy Nevill, writing in 1910, complained about the modern fashion for reducing the number of courses at meals, so that they comprised little more than "two entrees, soup, a little fish and a very light sweet". Was the writer of the Women's Page in the *Advertiser* one of those trying to reduce the number of courses? In September she wrote "soup, fish, entrée, joint, game, sweet and savoury suffice to any man". She advised against thick soups, and recommended against the traditional lobster sauce for turbot - a little melted butter with anchovy or egg yolk was better. She also disliked entrées that were too creamy: dentists advised chewing, so too much soft food wasn't healthy. As for wine, like most Edwardians she was unadventurous: sherry first, then claret or hock, followed by champagne.

Obviously these were meals to serve guests. More usually a meal consisted of meat and two vegetables followed by a pudding. Josephine Butler remembered that they ate very filling food. Some examples of typical meals from writers of the time:

- cold pork from Sunday with nice cold potatoes and pickle. Cold suet pudding with treacle, then cheese - pale, hard sort of cheese - with a jug of beer   *History of Mr Polly*

- bacon and broad beans and a macaroni pudding *Wind in the Willows*

- fried sprats - a treat for tea *The Old Century* Sassoon

Meat and two vegetables implies a joint of meat, but there were other parts of the animal to be eaten. *Mrs Beeton* included recipes for the following bits of a pig: cheek, ears, feet, fry (heart, lungs, liver, sweetbread), head, kidney and tongue. These would be eaten at luncheon or as entrées. The *Advertiser*, following the advice given above for turbot with anchovy sauce, included the following recipe for a 'nice dish' (Lamb's Brains and Tongue à la Creme):

Take a couple of lamb's tongues and stew them in a nicely flavoured stock. A qtr hour before they are cooked, add the brains from a couple of lamb's heads, tied in a muslin bag. After the qtr hour, remove the brains and tongues. Chop up the former with a little parsley; season; and return to the pan with a knob of butter rolled in flour. Stir until smooth. Skin the tongues and chop finely. Add to the brains with 4 tblspoons of thick cream. Work all together and serve with a border of spinach.

There was no use of pasta other than macaroni - as a milk pudding or with cheese - and it was boiled for 45 minutes before being baked. Frank Eling of St James' Park, remembered that there was always enough food in his family, though one only ate at meal-times - there was no picking of food from the larder in between. They were lucky to have a back-garden to grow vegetables.

Milk delivery cart in St James Rd.

Milk was delivered from hard-carts, the milk being poured from the churn into the customers jug, using a tin can. In some parts of town it was delivered twice a day. Without refrigeration it was difficult to keep fresh; in the summer it had to be boiled. Ice was available for those close to fishmongers, Tolson's, for example, on the Pantiles, or JJ Reading in Chapel Place, and could be used to make ice-cream. In one of her short stories, Sarah Grand talked of "that part of a sophisticated dinner party when the ice cream promotes thought by checking digestion".

It seems that eggs, and chickens, were, to some extent, seasonal - more plentiful in the spring. This may explain the various instructions given for preserving them - in three gallons of soft water, with a pint of fresh slaked lime and a pint of salt.

Other Events in October

Politics

There was no respite during October in the battle over the Budget, with both local papers strongly supporting their respective parties. The *Courier* described a Lloyd George speech as "unbridled violence"; and the *Advertiser*, a Lord Hardinge speech at the Opera House, as "vapid and inconsequential".

The increasing militancy of the suffragettes, as a result of forcible feeding by the authorities, saw an increase in local meetings against women's suffrage. At one of them, a Miss Fothergill explained it was because women were at heart largely Socialist, that she was opposed to giving them the vote. (Lloyd George opposed votes for women for the opposite reason - while the property qualification remained , the vote would go mainly to Conservative women.)

The increasing political tension spread to local elections, which were usually uncontested. The *Courier* urged all those who valued economical administration to abandon their usual apathy and vote at a South Ward election in October. In the event, the weather was bad, and turnout was low, but the Ratepayers' League candidate had a comfortable victory.

A New Skating Rink

Excitement was building through October over announcements of a new skating rink - the largest indoor rink outside London. A grand opening ceremony was planned for November 1st.

The Maharajah's Car

Both *Courier* and *Gazette* reported that the Maharajah of Bharatpur was staying at the Wellington, and had bought a magnificent 35hp FIAT landaulet. October 4th was the Maharajah's 10th birthday, so the car may have been a present. The story reminds us of the caricature of Tunbridge Wells as the home of ex-Indian Army officers and civil servants. It has been difficult to validate this stereotype. Certainly there are references, in obituaries for example, to a career in the Bombay or Madras Civil Service. But in a recent study of 'empire families' the author does not include Tunbridge Wells in her main list of Anglo-Indian** towns: Eastbourne, Cheltenham, other South Coast resorts and Bedford (attracted by the presence of suitable

** Anglo-Indian in the sense of British families who had worked in India.

schools). The difficulty is that in most sources: the census, directories, etc, there is little to distinguish them from other retired people. One possible source is a collection of 'Contemporary Biographies', prepared in 1900 of the most eminent residents of Kent. Forty one of these lived in Tunbridge Wells, and of those, ten had a direct connection with India. If we consider that perhaps half of the forty one were local families involved in trade, or the law, and that these hardly ever had an Indian connection; then the proportion of the remainder, which we might label the 'genteel' sector, with an Indian connection might be as high as 50%. It's a disappointingly vague estimate, and a subject that calls for further study.

Pluck and Endurance

AJ Sproston, the motor-cyclist from St John's, competed in the Isle of Man TT. A few minutes into the race the bike slipped into a ditch, crushing his left foot. Not realising that his ankle was broken, he pulled off his boot, and continued the race. He completed the 158 miles in just under 5 hours -finishing 18th out of 19. Lord Raglan, presenting the prizes, described it as a "remarkable instance of British pluck and endurance".

November

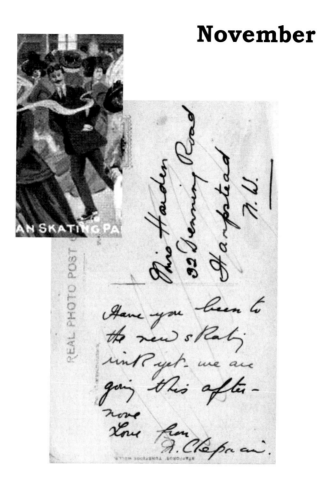

In which we consider:

- A Skating Palace and a new Theatre de-Luxe
- Treatment of Animals
- The new Mayor
- Vaughan Gower's Triumph

On November 1st, the town finally got the Skating Rink it felt it deserved. The new building, called the American Skating Palace, was in Culverden Down, between what is now Culverden Avenue and Whitefield Road. It replaced the Down Lane football ground. At 18,000 sq ft, it was at least six times as big as the Pump Room.

Despite its size, it couldn't cope with the numbers who turned up on the opening day. Those who managed to get in found a military band, attendants in neat military uniform, a corps of uniformed lads responsible for attaching the skates, and an "ingenious electrical contrivance that indicated to skaters the programme for the evening". (I cannot imagine what this might have been.)

Like the Pump Room, the Skating Palace was open in three sessions: morning, afternoon and evening. The morning session was free, the afternoon cost 1s, and the evening 6d. Skate hire was 1s. Monthly season tickets were available at 1 guinea. The Management had a strict 'no tipping' rule, 'à la Lyons', which the *Gazette* considered a most welcome innovation.

The Palace was backed by an American company which had already opened a rink in St Leonards. There were said to be 150 across the country. The manager, Mr RF Blackman, explained that no-one need be afraid of their children or wives going to the rink - it was not likely that they would be spoken to by strangers. The palace, he said, would be like a high-class ball-room.

The *Gazette* explained the benefits of the new activity: "as a graceful

The American Skating Palace in Culverden Down. Opened in November 1909

THE AMERICAN SKATING PALACE, TUNBRIDGE WELLS.

exercise, roller skating stands alone. The erect posture - for you must keep erect - developes the lungs by opening otherwise unused air cells, a beneficial result that is generally only achieved by strenuous exertions made in more violent forms of sport". It advised though that it was an activity for the winter only - too much indoor exercise in summer would be unpleasant.

The Palace organised skating races - a One-Mile Open Handicap was held on 2nd December. They promised that London's best skaters - the Aldwych Skating Club - would be attending. The race was organised over four heats and a final, and the winner, Mr W Soper, with a time of 3mins and 55 seconds, was indeed from the Aldwych club.

Faced with the competition of the American Skating Palace, the Pump Room reduced their prices and provided skates without charge, but soon accepted that they could not compete. On 12th November they announced a new attraction. The London Cinematographic Co was to commence a winter season at the Pump Room. It was to become a "place of amusement de-luxe", with carpets and tip-up velvet chairs.Only the highest class films would be shown, with the programme changing twice a week. I feel sure that it would not have matched the following description of cinemas at the time: "cinemas were filthy and smelly, and not just from the thick cigarette and pipe smoke that filled them ... they could be particularly foul-smelling after a screening to a full-house of children unable to contain their excitement" . As programmes were short the owners tended not to provide public conveniences; instead, attendants would walk through the aisles spraying the air from large bottles filled with bright blue Jeyes fluid.

*   *   *

The first winter meet of the Eridge Foxhounds was celebrated with photographs in the *Gazette* and *Courier*. They made three kills, the second after a very short run, which was considered rather unsporting of the fox. The Eridge was one of a number of hunts working the area: the West Kent Foxhounds, the Mid-Kent Staghounds, the Crowhurst Otter Hounds, and the Fordcombe and Hadlow Harriers.

Otter hunting had started earlier, in August, after an eight-week break to protect the hay. The Crowhurst pack met at Barden Park, near Tonbridge, and chased a large dog otter up the Powder Mill stream. He was heading for the safety of the Leigh Park lake, but they eventually got him after an hour and a quarter. It was "a capital morning's sport".

Hunting was reported as just another social and sporting activity, with often more than a hint of admiration for the participants. There was a story of the Hailsham Harriers, for example, from 1908. They had pursued an exhausted hare down to the sea-shore. The hare took to the water to escape. But the hunt wasn't to be cheated of its kill. One of the hunters, praised for his single-minded determination, stripped off and went in after him.

Some treatment of animals was condemned, like the boys who caught frogs in the Brighton Lake, and pulled their legs off. And there were court cases of ugly and senseless brutality, like the Southborough man who tied up his dog and threw bricks at it for half an hour. Most animal cruelty cases, and there were many of them, related to the uncaring attitude of those who worked with horses - typically taking them out when they already had open harness sores. It wasn't just the individual carter with only one animal who was to blame; in October the Omnibus Company was fined £2 for working a horse with a wound in its shoulder. Many of the witnesses were police officers who had previously worked with animals and could speak authoritatively on the subject. Then there were RSPCA inspectors, who were not always welcomed by animal owners. In May, a fly-proprietor in Dunstan Road threatened to throw the inspector down Dunstan Hill if he didn't get off his premises.

*   *   *

Frederick Wadham Elers

In November the town needed a new Mayor. There was no obvious successor to Cllr Caley, though there was a suggestion that he might continue for a second year, or that Alderman Woollan, Mayor in 1907 and 1908, might take the rôle again. Alderman Delves, long-serving Chairman of the Finance Committee, turned it down, and was made a Freeman of the Borough instead. A problem that might have influenced some councillors was the cost involved - hosting functions and contributing to appeals. Ultimately the councillors had to go outside of their number and offer it to Frederick Wadham Elers, Treasurer of the General Hospital. A keen sportsman in his youth, at 75 he was described as being in excellent health, though he was under medical orders not to attend evening meetings. As a student in the 1850's he coxed the Oxford boat.

The annual church service for the Corporation was held on November 14th. There should have been a formal procession from the Town Hall to Holy Trinity, with the Mayor and Alderman in their robes, accompanied by a detachment of police; but the weather was poor, so they went by car instead. Archdeacon Scott spoke to the text "Not slothful in business, fervent in spirit, serving the Lord". Attendance by the other councillors was poor. The *Gazette* considered this a regrettable tendency in modern life.

One of the Mayor's first duties was to speak at the County School for Girls, where he said they should be taught shorthand and typing instead of music and French. Here was someone who believed in a woman's right to work, albeit in a limited rôle**.

A much younger politician was also in the news in November. Robert Vaughan Gower was a 29 year-old solicitor, and one of the rising

** Though these were not exclusively female skills. The majority of those studying shorthand and typing at the Technical Institute were boys.

young stars of the local Conservative party. He was interviewed by *Society* in March, but he gave very little away, much to the frustration of the reporter, who said he showed a "most religious reticence". He lived at 23 Ferndale, a fine four-bedroomed house bought for £2,200 earlier in the year**.

Gower had grown up in Calverley Street. His father, Joshua Gower, had been a house agent, and a councillor, and had amassed a property empire across the smaller streets of the East Ward. He was a paternalistic landlord, hosting a dinner for his elderly tenants each year. Joshua died in 1907. Robert took over the family trusts, and sought to build on his father's popularity. When he married in 1907, he was presented with an address and handsome gift by 200 of his tenants.

Robert Gower had long been involved in local politics. At 16, he was Assistant Hon. Secretary of the Ratepayers' League, and as a recently qualified solicitor in the mid 1900's, he had campaigned against the Council's plans to buy the chalybeate spring from the Lord of the Manor. In 1904 he had been defeated in a South Ward election by only seven votes. When Cllr Wesley Smith resigned his seat in the East Ward in November 1909, Gower was put forward in his place. Jim Richards of Camden Road stood against him. After the socialist victory in the East Ward earlier in the month (see page 187) it promised to be a closely-run fight.

Gower published his manifesto in the *Courier*. He affirmed his opposition to 'municipal trading' and the waste of ratepayers' money on speculative undertakings. He also stressed his connections with the East Ward - he had lived in it, or near it, all his life. He emphasised the need to tackle unemployment, by imaginative policies, like recruiting only local people, and awarding contracts to local firms only.

It could have been a closely-run contest, but it wasn't. Gower had

** He also owned 27, Ferndale, bought the previous December for £1,700.

136

the resources - 20 to 30 cars available to ferry supporters to the polling station. He had the loyalty of his tenants. He had the contacts that he had built up over the years (he was, for example, a founder member of the Camden Road Conservative Working Men's Club (at no 141)). On polling day his baby daughter was wheeled around the ward with a placard "Vote for Daddy".

There was an 80% turnout. Gower got 903 votes, Richards 321. It was the highest total ever achieved for the Ward, possibly for the entire Council.After the results were announced at the Parish Room in Albion Road there was a gasp of amazement, then cheer after cheer. Richards got up to speak and was received in silence. Then there were calls for him to get his hair cut, and eventually he was drowned out. Gower was carried shoulder-high to the Conservative Committee Room and then around the streets of the Ward. He was accompanied by a crowd of several hundred, singing "See the Conquering Hero Comes".

Other Events of November

Shackleton's Visit

Shackleton's promised visit came on November 4th, with two talks at the Great Hall. A 'lady resident' wrote him a poem. She didn't give her name, which is understandable when you read it. Here is the first verse:

> Back from the land of ice and snow
> And across the Antarctic track
> He furthest South with his crew did go
> Now, he has safely brought them back

The Last Climbing Boy

Mr George Baker, at 77 the town's oldest sweep, died in November. He had started as a climbing boy, aged 6.

Working Girls

Amelia Scott, the Poor Law Guardian (see page 121), was active in other ways. In 1900 she had been one of the founders of a club for 'working girls'. By 1909 it was called 'The Leisure Hour Club for Young Women in Business', and had premises at 136 Upper Grosvenor Road. For a quarterly subscription of 1/-, the thirty or so members could attend on Sundays and two evenings a week, and enjoy outings and entertainments. It was intended to provide young women with an alternative to some of the less suitable attractions in the town. In November the committee was considering whether Morris Dancing would be popular.

Education Committee

There were complaints in November about the composition of the Borough Education Committee, specifically about the number of unelected members (seven out of fifteen) for a committee with a budget of £16,000. Having co-opted members allowed the Council to insist that there were always at least two women members. (It also took care to ensure that there were never more than three.)

A Question of Title

A resident of one of the town's boarding houses was annoyed that his newsagent addressed letters to him as Mr, rather than Esq. His first complaint having been ignored, he sent the newsagent a long letter explaining why he felt justified in demanding his preferred appellation. It was perhaps mean of the newsagent to forward the letter to the *Advertiser*, and mean of the *Advertiser* to print it, but what a perfect example it was of the pompous attitudes that gave the town, and country, such a bad name. "I am not an upstart or retired tradesman, but have been independent all my life and my father and grandfather before me." He gave no evidence of having achieved or contributed anything that would justify enhanced respect, basing his claim of the fact that his sister had married a ship-owner, and his brother was a graduate.

House of Lords

On 30th November the House of Lords rejected Lloyd George's Budget. The country prepared for a General Election.

December

From a business card of FD Davies.
Tailor and breeches maker. 6 Kentish Buildings

In which we consider:

- The Death of Woollan

- The Ideal Man

- Christmas Preparations

Benjamin Minors Woollan lived at Sherwood Park in Pembury Road. He had been Mayor in 1907 and 1908, and remained closely involved in the administration of the town, as Alderman and JP.

Early in November he caught a chill while out shooting on the estate. He missed the banquet for the new mayor - and was himself missed at the banquet, as his light-hearted banter with Paget Hedges the previous year had lessened the political tension between the Liberal MP and the largely Conservative Council. The chill developed into pleurisy and pneumonia and he died on December 5th.

Mr. B. M. Woollan.

Woollan was born in New Brunswick (Canada) but made his money in South Africa. A year after gold was discovered on the Witwatersrand in 1886, 30 year-old Woollan founded what was to become the Johannesburg Stock Exchange. He came to Tunbridge Wells in about 1901, and bought Sherwood from the widow of Sir William Siemens. He became involved in many aspects of life in the town, especially those involved with sport: cricket, football, rifle-shooting, and was President of the new Grove Bowls Club, founded in 1909. A quote from the Town football club demonstrates both his character and his humour: "Now, boys, pull together for my sake. I hate to be identified with a failure."

Woollan was a great Nelson enthusiast. On Trafalger Day, October 21st, he displayed the famous message 'England expects ...' from Sherwood Park. It was also displayed at the Town Hall - Woollan having donated the necessary flags during his spell as Mayor. The Town Hall held a more valuable Nelson memento - the 'memorandum' by which Nelson explained his plan of attack for what was to be the Battle of Trafalgar. The details were copied and communicated to each captain in the fleet. Woollan bought the original document, in Nelson's hand-writing, in 1906, for £3,600, to be presented to the British Museum on his death. In the meantime it was held at the Town Hall for display to residents and visitors. Woollan designed an explanatory pamphlet which was printed by J Newns of Calverley

Road. The memorandum is now held by the British Library, and may be seen on its web-site (and a copy of the pamphlet is held by the University of California, and may be seen on its web-site).

*　　　*　　　*

Earlier in the year the *Advertiser* described its 'Perfect Woman' (see page 50). It then considered its 'Ideal Man':

" First of all he must be a gentleman ... gentleness and moral strength combined ... the polish that only comes from association with those so happily placed that they have enjoyed education and refinement throughout their lives. He must be thoughtful to others, kind to women and children, and all helpless things, tender-hearted to the old, and the poor, and the unhappy, but never foolishly weak."

The writer recognised that many young men did not have have these advantages, and had to leave home before learning the social niceties. In a series of articles she provided guidance to them.

- on meeting an acquaintance

If it be a male friend, then a nod is sufficient. If it is an older man, then it might be advisable to raise the hat. If the acquaintance is with a lady; or if the young man is himself with a lady "even if she be only a mother or sister", then the hat must be raised. The young man must only put out a hand to shake if a lady has indicated that she expects it. "This is a test of good breeding that is constantly applied".

- while out walking

Whistling and singing are incompatible with the conduct of a gentleman in the street (though they are permitted in a quiet country lane). Nor is it permitted to wear the hands in the pockets in city streets - this is one reason for carrying a cane or umbrella.

- accidental encounters

Should a young gentleman be fortunate enough to perform some service to a young lady, eg picking up a parcel or sunshade, he must raise his hat and retire. This must not be taken as an excuse for an introduction. Some women may do this deliberately - it need hardly be said that these are hardly ever gentlewomen. Girls of the lower middle class are prone to it, and many men in cities have no women acquaintances to otherwise effect introductions, but a man must be wary of choosing as a wife, a girl who has shown so little discretion.

- offering an umbrella

As to whether a gentleman should offer the use of his umbrella to a

141

lady - no true lady would accept the offer from a stranger.

- seaside encounters

The seaside season seems to encourage these encounters, 'flirtations' almost, as does bicycling. If a young man should meet a girl in this way, he should treat her as he would like his sister to be treated. And he must be wary of accepting an invitation from a young woman where he has not been introduced to her family. A horse-whipping is not a pretty sight.

- a first dinner party

A young man must not expect to be given a pretty girl to 'take down' at his first dinner party - these are reserved for men with more social experience. He will probably be assigned an unmarried lady of uncertain age, however these are usually excellent for practising on. When going down to dinner, the gentleman offers the arm which will place them on the wall side of the stairs. If the dining room is on the same floor, he offers the right arm.

- in the dining room

It is old-fashioned good manners to wait until everybody is served - so old-fashioned that it only survives among uncultured people - the correct thing to do is to start without reference to others. You will be offered a second helping of soup, but you must never take it, nor of the fish. Dishes are presented to the left side of the diner, who serves himself with his right-hand. Nobody is expected to eat all the courses, but check the menu beforehand as you will not be told what is being served, and you must not hesitate in making a decision. Celery, asparagas, and cheese straws are eaten with the fingers; oranges with a knife and fork. Cheese is usually eaten on bread, though a few still follow the old practice of eating it from the knife.

*   *   *

Piano suppliers had been reminding readers of the approach of Christmas since September, and on 12th November Colonel Pulley of Speldhurst had complained of carol-singers; but it wasn't until early December that the Christmas advertising really began. Noakes was prominent early in the month, but was soon joined by Weekes, Dust's, Philpot's, Goldsmith's and others. Waymark's advertised its linens "so dear to the heart of the housewife", and said that maids should not be forgotten, with dress lengths, caps and aprons.

In 1908 *Society* was claiming that Christmas was changing - that one ate out on Christmas Day, that even when eating at home, the plum pudding would be bought. Certainly one could buy a Christmas pudding - price 8d, but I doubt that many families ate out on Christmas Day. The final week before Christmas saw the papers full of adverts for local butchers: in the High St, Pantiles, Chapel Place, Mount Pleasant, Grosvenor Road, Calverley and Camden Roads. Not just turkey, but beef, mutton, geese, pheasants, rabbits and hares, and, in St James Road, country-fed pork. Semple's in Calverley Road laid on the Borough Band from 7 to 9pm on the Tuesday before Christmas.

The skating rink was popular throughout the month. There was a fancy dress carnival on the 15th, 200 attended in costume, with nearly 1,000 spectators. The fun continued until 2am in the High Street afterwards, as the photographer Doyle Rowe took portraits of the winners. In Tonbridge the Council discussed proposals for a rink, and was pressurised to ignore the advice of the Borough Surveyor that the plans were against the local bye-laws. On New Year's Eve the Culverden rink held a 'Grand Skating Cinderella', from 7:30 to midnight. Evening dress was compulsory until 10pm, though ladies were advised that a train was not mandatory, and perhaps not advisable. Customers were assured that the rink was now cosy and warm with gas heaters.

Over the Christmas period the local Post Office handled over two and a half million letters and cards, 54,000 parcels, nearly 15,000 telegrams and 4,000 trunk telephone calls. One of the cards was of the Pantiles, sent to 'My Dear Lettie', from her brother. He wishes her a Very Happy Xmas and Prosperous New Year, and goes on:

> And now my dearest Sister
> We both are growing old
> With Christmas fast approaching
> And not yet in the Fold
> Oh how it would our hearts rejoice
> If we should hear you say
> That through the precious Blood of Christ
> I've found the Living Way

On 15th December Evan Jenkin Lloyd visited his wife. She gave him a sovereign. On 24th December the papers reported his death in a Clerkenwell hotel. He had taken cyanide.

*   *   *

A new leader was appointed to the local Salvation Army in November. In December he come across a boy in a shop trying to buy a pennyworth of pea flour. He followed him home and found a respectable workman and his wife, out of work for six weeks, trying to feed a family of six children on 6/- a week. To Adjutant Brogdale this was an example of the "genuine need often hid behind the garb of dignified respectability. These dear children were not ragged or dirty, neither do they beg door to door. We have resolved that they must be helped."

But how best to help the unemployed was not clear. A committee of councillors had reported in October, saying that simply providing relief was unproductive. They put forward proposals, based on the latest advice from the Poor Law Commission, that emphasis should be placed not on charity, but on generating work by applying public funds to worthwhile projects. The proposal was heavily defeated and a new scheme very much like the old one was introduced instead. By December the new Mayor was appealing for funds, and unemployment processions and collections had started again (and were generating the same complaints as the previous year). This year the problem was worse. The Committee of the Boot Fund felt that the economic situation was such that it would not be worth making a public appeal. In response to this news, the headmaster of High Brooms school appealed directly to the public for second-hand boots.

The West Ward

(part 1)

- **The Brighton Station**

- **Broadwater Down**

- **Ye Pantiles**

- **High Street and Mount Sion**

Please see map on page 202.

The Four Wards

When the Borough of Tunbridge Wells was created in 1889, it was divided into four wards: North, East, South and West. The primary objective in defining the ward boundaries was to ensure that each ward had a similar number of voters (called 'burgesses'). The map-makers were very successful in this: the numbers across the four wards varied only between 1095 and 1194. The wards however, differed in geographical size, and in relative wealth. Using 1889 rateable values as an indication, we can calculate the relative wealth of the four wards (North, East, South and West) at 20%, 15%, 25% and 40% of the total**.

It is not surprising that the West Ward was the most wealthy. It contained the core of the old town: the Pantiles, the High Street and Mount Sion, the Common and Mount Ephraim, and many of the more exclusive 19th century developments: Broadwater Down, Nevill and Hungershall Parks. In this chapter we will consider the eastern half of the West Ward, what we might term the Old Town.

The Brighton Station

We start at what was then called the Brighton Station - it didn't become the West Station until 1923. It was operated by the London, Brighton and South Coast Railway Company (LB&SCR) - you could

** Fifty years later changes in the franchise meant that the number of voters had increased more than fourfold, but virtually the same division of wealth applied: 22%, 17%, 24% and 37%.

get trains from there to London, Brighton and the South Coast. There were 13 trains to London (Victoria) on weekdays, with four on Sunday. It took about an hour and a half. There were 12 to Brighton and seven to Eastbourne. The Eastbourne route went through Mayfield and Heathfield and took about an hour and a half with ten intermediate stations. The journey to Brighton took about an hour and 20 minutes, and went via Crowborough, Uckfield and Lewes.

There was a new station-master in 1909, Mr William Norman, who had started in the goods office in Worthing 37 years earlier. There was an article about him in *Society*, with a picture and details of his career and hobbies: gardening and poultry keeping. A station-master was an important figure in the commercial life of the town. His social standing, however, is indicated by the following snippet from EM Forster's *A Room with a View*. Miss Bartlett has asked George Emerson what his profession was, and he has answered 'the railway'. She is horrified. She had no idea that it would be such a dreadful answer, or she would never have asked him. The tactful Mr Beebe changes the subject.

In front of the station was Nevill Terrace leading down to the Carlton Hotel. The terrace had been intended as residential property to be let as apartments, but ten years earlier Thomas Bates had moved into no. 6. Bates was setting up as a builder and built a workshop in the back garden. The noise of hammering and sawing from 6 in the morning until the evening drove away the other tenants. In 1907 Bates took over nos. 7 and 8 as offices, and eventually bought nos. 5, 6, 7, 8 and 14.

To the west of the station was the Agricultural Showground. To the east was the relatively recent (1890's) development of Linden Park (see right). A Guide Book of the time described the residents as: retired merchants, widows and maiden

ladies of independent means, unbeneficed clergymen, and gentlemen who have served their country in the army, navy or in colonial appointments.

Broadwater Down

Beyond Linden Park and Frant Road were the older and grander houses of Broadwater Down, built in the 1860's by George Mansfield and one of the most select parts of town. The census provides little information on the residents, other than that they typically had five or more servants; but there are tantalising hints elsewhere of Slatin Pasha and Reginald Wingate, Governor-General of the Sudan**. Broadwater Down was lined with a double row of lime trees. Unfortunately by 1909 their roots were causing problems. In December the Council was faced with an estimate of £2,000 for renewing the sewers.

Until 1894 Broadwater Down and Frant Road were in Frant parish in Sussex. In that year they were transferred to the new borough of Tunbridge Wells, and to the county of Kent. They remained within Sussex, though, for the 1901 census, and within the Rye Parliamentary constituency; and St Mark's Church continued to be in the Diocese of Chichester (where it remained until 1991). The Rev JH Townsend was very proud of St Mark's - the first in Tunbridge Wells to have electric lighting. It was also the first in England (outside

** Slatin Pasha was an Austrian who served as Governor of Darfur under General Gordon. He was held captive by the 'mahdi's forces for 11 years. Wingate, an intelligence officer at the time arranged his rescue.

FIRESIDE SERMONS.

of London and Birmingham) to use the Electrophone. This was a system for broadcasting sermons (or speeches or concerts) using the domestic telephone network. A microphone was positioned near the pulpit, and the sermon transmitted to the telephone exchange. Subscribers to the Electrophone service would connect to the exchange using specialised receivers and hear the sermon. The system was first demonstrated in 1892 and survived until the spread of radio in the 1920's. Mr Townsend told the story of one parishioner, too ill to attend church, who nevertheless was able to listen to one of his services by Electrophone, and sent off a cheque for £10 to Dr Barnardo's which he had mentioned in the sermon.

To modern eyes the view of Frant Road, below, is idyllic. To one resident, a letter writer to the *Courier* throughout May and June, it was a nightmare. The problem was dust: "gardens and lawns are destroyed, house ventilation cannot be obtained under the penalty of furniture being smothered in road grit". As the horse excreta dried and was pulverised by passing wheels, its dust hung in the air - to the detriment of the health of invalids and visitors in bath-chairs. The writer called on the Council to tar the road, or at least to increase the frequency at which it was watered.

To the east of Frant Road were the new developments of Madeira and Warwick Parks - over 100 detached and semi-detached houses, most less than ten years old.

Ye Pantiles

Approaching the Pantiles from the Brighton Station, along Eridge Road, the first major building was the Pump Room. This had opened in 1877. It had two spacious rooms on the ground floor at the front, and a much larger room, 36' by 60' behind (see below). Initially visitors had used it as a lounge for reading the papers and taking  the waters but both had been cut off by 1909. The building was still occasionally used for Balls and Masonic events, and for weekly meetings of the Farmers' Club, but, as a business, it was moribund and went into liquidation during the year.

 The Pump Room was replaced by Union Square in the 1960's but most of the rest of the Pantiles looked broadly similar to what it does today. There were daily band concerts during the summer, with rows of seats around the bandstand. There were visitors in bathchairs, old ladies dressed in black, men with bowler hats and women with parasols. The *Advertiser* considered it narrow and stuffy, especially for evening performances. The area behind the Great Hall had been suggested as a possible alternative. The *Advertiser* preferred a sunken bandstand on the common, as in Margate, but recognised that this would mean dealing with the Lord of the Manor, "a personage who does not seem to be overwhelmingly in love with the town". There was quite a history behind this statement - Frank Baird, Lord of the Manor of Rusthall, was a very difficult character. In the early 1890's he had objected to the Council installing public conveniences

on the Pantiles, even though property owners confirmed that previously "streams of urine could almost at any time be seen running across the Promenade". In 1909 he challenged the right of the Council to replace gas lights with electric. He claimed the right to vet the new designs - the Council disagreed.

One difference between 1909 and 2008 was the type of shops on the Pantiles. There were many more drapers and outfitters, Dust's being perhaps the most notable. In February they advertised the 'most important corset exhibition ever held in Tunbridge Wells'. There was a bank, and there were food shops: grocers, butchers, bakers, a dairy, and, in the Olde Fish-Market, a fishmonger. There was a weekly market in the Corn Exchange. The Royal Sussex Hotel had become a furniture repository. Back in 1886 it had had to seek formal permission to use the Royal title.

This was granted on the basis that it was of long standing.

Finally we might suggest that the Pantiles, or more precisely, Major York's Road, was the red-light district of Tunbridge Wells. In three cases of prostitution brought before the bench in 1909, the 'action' had taken place there.

The High Street

The appearance of the High Street too would be broadly familiar to today's shoppers. Indeed many of the traders' names are still recognisable in the town: Bracketts, Goulden & Curry, Paynes, Farrers, Breeds, Saltmarsh, and, in Chapel Place, Hall's bookshop. Some of the shops have gone: there were, for example, four coal merchants in the High Street in 1909; and Wray's Umbrella Manufactory in Vale Road is no more. Mr Wray, sad to say, died in June 1909 on a visit to Gloucester. The High Street was popular with dentists: the London Teeth Co. at no. 32 and Bradlaw Philips, American Dentists at 33. At least these were on opposite sides of the road. Shipley-Slipper and Ernest Francis were next door at nos. 10 and 12. Both of them included anguished requests in their adverts that clients carefully check the name-plate before entering.

22747. Tun ridge Wells. High Street and Christ-Church.

Mount Sion

What we might nowadays call the 'village area', ie that part between the High Street, Mount Sion and the Grove was very much a working class area in 1909 - home to engine drivers, postmen, gas fitters, coachmen, together with small shopkeepers, music teachers, tailors and the like. It was probably too expensive for the least well paid - there were few labourers, if any, as heads of household. There was, though, a 'common lodging house' in Little Mount Sion, which provided beds for 30 single men - labourers, pedlars, musicians, some building workers**. The address, no. 14, also seems to have contained a beer-house, mineral water manufacturer, house furnisher, and blacksmith's forge.

The population on the periphery was also mixed. Six of the first 15 houses on the left-hand side going up Mount Sion were lodging houses. Alderman WH Delves at 23, and the Weekes family at 25 are recognisably pillars of the community, but the rest are a mixture of traders, tradesmen, and people living on their own means. At 11 Cumberland Walk, going a little way out of the area, there was a 54 year-old 'billiard marker', which I think meant somebody who kept

** These details come from 1901 rather than 1909, but they should provide a guide to 1909. Of the 30 lodgers, three-quarters were 40 and over, and only 8 were local.

the score at billiards. His 24 year-old son followed the same profession.

On the right going up Mount Sion was the Eye and Ear Hospital (the present Fairlawn House). Until 1900 it had been the High School for Girls. Opposite, just on the left along Berkeley Road, was the Murray House School which educated girls and young boys from King Charles. This was at the top of Murray Road - what is currently called Frog Lane.

Berkeley Road was also the base for John Brown Dairies. This had been started more than 30 years earlier by the young John Brown and had prospered over the years, owning farms at Ramslye and Culverden. In 1909 it was trading as South of England Dairies. Mr Brown was elected a Councillor for the South Ward in 1905.

John Brown

Charity begins at Home

In March a number of ladies and gentlemen from the West Ward offered to subscribe further funds for the unemployed, on condition that they were used for the benefit of the unemployed within the West Ward. The offer was rejected, on the initiative of the Mayor I think, on the basis that any such funds should be used for the town as a whole.

The West Ward

(part 2)

- **London Road**

- **Hotels and Boarding Houses**

- **Mount Ephraim**

- **The Common**

Please see map on page 202.

London Road

The second part of the West Ward, the area around the Common, was the part of town most favoured by visitors. Standing opposite the church of King Charles the Martyr, the view was of the Grand Hotel (see opposite). The building dates from 1878, and was by local architect William Barnsley Hughes. It is an imposing building with impressive internal features, but it is small and it was not a commercial success. In the late 1880's, the leaseholder sued the builders for fraudulent representations about its finances. It was originally the Royal Kentish Hotel, became the Grand in 1904, but disappears from the directories by 1916. Today it is Kentish Mansions. In 1901 it had a very cosmopolitan staff: the manager was Hungarian, two of the waiters were German, and a third Swedish; and there were Dutch and Swedish staff in the kitchen.

In contrast, the staff at the Castle Hotel (below) were resolutely British, in keeping with its traditional ethos. *Society* summarised the attractions of the various hotels in the town. Visitors chose the Spa for its size and unique surroundings, and the Calverley for its exclusiveness and 'county' clientele. The Wellington was modern and up-to-date, while the Castle represented homely comfort, with its creeper-covered exterior and fifteen bow windows, and art treasures in every room. The Castle proprietor, William Urquhart, provided catering for events at the Opera House.

Between the Castle Hotel and the Vale Royal Methodist Church

was the Harewood House Boarding Establishment, advertised as having "Electric Light throughout. Separate Tables. Every Comfort". It was only the first, though possibly the biggest, of many such establishments facing the Common along London Road and Mount Ephraim.

Tunbridge Wells 1909 - Boarding Houses & Apartments

from The Tunbridge Wells Gazette and Fashionable Visitor List
(this is by no means an exhaustive list)

London Road
Harewood House
Heath Villa
Tweeddale Terrace 3
Ritz House
Richmond Terr 1-3
Vale Royal 1-2
Balmoral
Vale Towers (BH)
Sandringham
Clarence House
The Common
Sandown Place
Summerhill House
Holmbrook

Howrah House
Stellenburg
Deep de
Limehill House
Rock Villa
Mount Ephraim Road
Victoria House
Apsley House
Marston Lodge
Osborne House
Napier Mansions
Rockmount
Oldenburgh House
Mount Ephraim
Sidney Place

Shirley Place
Hillbrow
Montpellier Lodge
Bella Vista
Belle Vue
Plaisance
Ratieff (BH)
Boyne House
Wellington Place
Fernhill
Rosemount
Ernstein House
Pavilion
Sussex House (BH)

A Selection of Apartments and Boarding Houses slightly away from Common.

Molyneux Park Mansions Private Hotel.

Norfolk Hotel (Church Road) - used this name from 1909.

Lonsdale Mansions "High-Class Apartment House. Over thirty Bedrooms and Private Sitting Rooms. Excellent Cuisine"

Tunbridge Wells and Counties Club, 1909. This sketch is from the architect's own files. The 'cupola' was added later in pencil.
Picture reproduced by permission of Burns Guthrie and partners

A significant addition to London Road in 1909 was the Tunbridge Wells & Counties Club (see above). The building was designed by Cecil Burns, a young local architect, and built by Beale & Sons. The cost was said to be in five figures.

The facilities included a coffee room, reading room, and billiard saloon on the ground floor; and a card room and "magnificent" smoking room on the first floor. The Tunbridge Wells Club had been based in the Great Hall for 30 years, but accommodation there was limited. In making the move, the name was changed to encourage new 'country' members. Candidates for membership had to be proposed by existing members and approved by the Committee. The entrance fee was 5 guineas, with an annual subscription of 4 guineas. Visitors could apply for temporary membership.

The space vacated in the Great Hall was taken over in 1910 by the newly-formed Kent and Sussex Club. This may have been a resurrection of the old Nevill Club, which had been based in the Pump Room since 1878, but which had been wound up in December 1909.

Mount Ephraim

That the Common was to Tunbridge Wells what the Ocean was to other resorts, is a commonplace, but I had not previously heard of Mount Ephraim being likened to the Rialto. *Society* in January 1909 claimed this was a common usage, then complained that it was not being patronised after morning church as in former times, as so many fashionable families were wintering abroad. The phrase 'South of France', though, is documented by both Joan Burslem and Richard Cobb, and referred, I believe, to a sheltered part of Bishop's Down Road facing the Spa Hotel, much favoured by elderly residents of the Wellington.

There is something of a puzzle about the Spa Hotel. In none of the 1909 papers did I find any reference to the hotel offering anything more than billiards, golf, concerts and comfortable rooms. Did it still offer anything in the way of a spa? The *Advertiser* suggested not - in responding to the King's rejection of the label 'Kentish Spa', it said that there was little justification in the town using the word 'spa'. I was re-assured therefore by an article about the Spa Hotel in *Society* for December 1908, which listed the Turkish Spray Douche and Plunge Pool; the recently added Russian Bath and masseur; and the new electric light bath. This last seems to have been some form of sun lamp, and had wonderful curative properties:

Walking in Rusthall Road outside the Spa Hotel. The day looks gloomy but the lady in the front is carrying a sun-shade. A sun-tan was not considered appropriate for ladies until the 1920's.

"those physical infirmities that have come on through the natural currents of the blood becoming impaired, can be restored to their normal tone and power by means of the truly marvellous discovery of electricity applied in the form of radient heat."

The Wellington Hotel (see above) was closed for two months for refurbishment, but re-opened in May with a special luncheon for journalists from the London papers. They were most impressed by the views - over three counties. The views were obviously one of the attractions when two extra stories and a tower were added to Earl's Court when it was converted into a hotel in 1904

Between and behind the hotels were ordinary homes. One of the biggest was Chancellor House, the home since 1904 of Rachel Beer. From a very wealthy family herself, she had married Frederick Beer, owner of *The Observer* in 1887. In 1893 she bought the *Sunday Times*, and for a few years, while leading a glittering life in London society, she edited both newspapers. Frederick died in 1903, and Rachel suffered a breakdown. She withdrew from public life to Tunbridge Wells, under the care of a Miss Ross. I have come across only two references to her in 1909 - a subscription to Cricket Week, and one to the Leisure Hours Club for young women in business.

The northern slope of Mount Ephraim, away from the Common, had seen major changes in the 20 years prior to 1909 with the development of the Molyneux and Boyne Park estates. By 1909 there were more than 120 new houses - "good-class private residences for the comfortable classes", many designed by Caley.

The Common

In early June the *Evening Standard* printed a large article describing the attractions of Tunbridge Wells. It is probably not unfair to suggest that much of the material had been provided by the Advertising Association. The description started with a comment about how many trees there were in the town, yet one of the features most noticeable to modern eyes, is the lack of trees on the Common - due to grazing by cattle and sheep (see below).

The Common appealed to visitors, but was also a resource much used by residents. At one extreme it was a place of work - for the carpet-beaters, who, in the days before vacuum cleaners, cleaned carpets, and blankets, by hanging them between trees, and beating them with besoms. It was also the site of the Whitsun Bank Holiday Fair. The weather, unusually for 1909, was good that weekend, so many took the train to the coast. For those who stayed there, were swings, and roundabouts, and Aunt Sally's, and a refreshment tent manned by the British Women's Temperance Association. Josephine Butcher, who lived on the Pantiles, remembered how lovely the Fair looked in the evening with the coloured lights and lamps hanging over the stalls, and the music going on long after she had gone to bed.

TUNBRIDGE WELLS. — Back of Pantiles. — LL.

The Suffragettes held open-air meetings in the summer months. The *Advertiser* described a meeting in June in its usual disparaging way: "Mrs Despard and her faithful feminine followers experienced some difficulty in finding a suitable spot. Being women, of course, they were particular about such details, and close upon half an hour was spent ... in leading her audience about from one spot to another." The *Courier* reports it differently, explaining that they were seeking to meet the requirements of the by-laws that meetings be held a certain distance from public roads. The

speaker having found a suitable spot, the *Advertiser* went on: "The usual arguments against the 'tyranny' of man over women were set forth, and ... the usual interruptions added a spice of life to what would otherwise have been a dull repetition of hackneyed suffragette and socialistic phrase and rhetoric."

The Common could be dangerous. In April, 8 year old Arthur Slydel died after being hit on the head by a stone while listening to the Salvation Army band. At the next Council meeting, the Police were ordered to prosecute all stone throwers. There was a complaint in June about Socialists holding meetings on the Common with their usual tirade against King, and Government, and children attending Empire Day demonstrations. It echoed similar complaints from the TWTA in 1908. And there were complaints about the mess that was being made by the unemployed who were being paid to cut the furze.

The most contentious item, though, was the new, covered shelter - a TWTA project that seemed to infuriate the Ratepayers' League. A letter in August spoke of "absurd follies such as the hideous, useless shelters on our beautiful Common", while another complained of it being used by "lazy young urchins".

The South-Eastern Station

The South Eastern station as it may still have appeared at the beginning of 1909. Reproduced by kind permission of Tunbridge Wells Museum and Art Gallery'

The years around 1909 saw many changes to the South Eastern station and its surroundings. In 1907, the Borough Council and railway company replaced the old bridge over the railway. In 1912 they rebuilt the station building on the 'down' side, installing the current clock tower. Work in 1909 on the 'up' side has been less well documented, but it may well have involved the removal of the original 1847 colonnade (see above). In the words of the Courier, "although considered an architectural feature when the station was erected many years ago [it] has now become something of an obstruction". The two 'wings', by which the main building jutted out at first floor level, were also removed. At the same time, the 'up' platform was widened and given a new glass roof, and two new entrances provided to handle the extra passengers -typically 300 of them - who used the cheap trains on Wednesdays. And the footbridge was glazed - "to enhance protection from the weather and do away with the nuisance of loiterers".

The Advertising Association worked hard with the railway companies to advertise the town. Reports were received of posters advertising Tunbridge Wells seen in Hexham, Ripon, York and Harrogate. In July a "Sunny South Special" railway service was announced. This left Liverpool on weekdays at 11am, and travelled via Manchester, Stockport and Rugby, to Kensington and through to the Hastings line.

The South Ward

- **Grove Hill Road and St Peter's**

- **Mount Pleasant**

- **Calverley Road**

- **'Behind the Town Hall'**

- **Calverley Park Gardens and Pembury Road**

Please see map on page 203.

Grove Hill Road and St Peter's

We start our tour of the South Ward on the new railway bridge by the South Eastern station, built two years earlier in 1907. Facing us is the corner block which Weeke's (now Hooper's) would eventually take over completely. In 1909 it had a number of different occupants. On the corner itself was the Railway Bell hotel (see below), then, to the left, Weekes'

main drapery store, then the Bridge Hotel (see above), then Weekes' footwear and tailoring departments. To the right of the Bell, in Grove Hill Road, was Weekes' furniture department.

Going up Grove Hill Road (below), the *Advertiser* offices were on the right, and those of the *Courier* on the left. The town's original roller skating rink, some 25 years earlier, had been on the left - an area occupied by printers, photographers, and a riding school in 1909. The roads on the right leading through to the

166

Grove were well-established, those beyond the Grove, ie Grecian, Norfolk and Buckingham, were more recent, resulting from the development of the Claremont Park Estate in the 1880's. At the top of Grove Hill, Poona Road, its name redolent of the British in India, was built in the 1830's and 1840's. In 1909 most of it was owned by the South Eastern Railway and occupied by railway workers. Beyond Poona Road was the Girls' High School, and then Camden Park, which had developed slowly over a period of sixty years.

The area around St Peter's (see right) had been developed some forty years earlier. It was the home of Miss Bartlett in Forster's *A Room with a View*, a 'genteel' and most tiresome creature (she was the Maggie Smith character in the  film). What would she have thought of Edwin Skewis? He died of a heart attack in no 6 Cambridge Street, one Sunday afternoon in October. Mr Skewis lived in Rusthall. His wife lived in Upper Grosvenor Road. Emily Tozer lived at no 6 Cambridge St. On the Sunday in question he drank a bottle of whisky, and died shortly afterwards, falling down a couple of steps in the house.

Mount Pleasant

Returning to the railway bridge and looking to the left, up Mount Pleasant, we would have seen the squat, old tower of the 'down' platform (see opposite). Across the road was the Great Hall, very similar in overall shape and appearance to what it is today, though in 1909 it actually contained a great hall, used for concerts and dinners, and by the Post Office at Christmas for collecting and sorting parcels. Behind the Great Hall, the Calverley Grounds were private, only made available to the public for special events, for example during Cricket Week. There were no shops on the left-hand side of the hill, just the garden walls of four large houses occupied by doctors and solicitors. The right-hand side though, had shops much as today.

Amongst them were those of Frederick Wickham, draper, who started in 1899 with no. 21, then went on to acquire nos. 27, 23, 24 and 25. Plate-glass windows were a feature, and telephones in every department. At the

top was Lloyds Bank (see opposite). Until 1890 it had been Beechings, a private bank with branches in Tonbridge and Hastings.

Across the junction where we now have the Town Hall, the Library and the Assembly Hall, were the sturdy sandstone blocks of Calverley Parade, Calverley Mount and Calverley Terrace, built by Decimus Burton in the 1830's. Calverly Mount (see below) stood across the angle of the corner, like the current Town Hall. Vaughan Gower, the solicitor, had his office here.

Calverley Parade, to the left, was on the line of the current library and museum; Calverley Terrace, to the right, lay back from the road, with lawns in front.

Beyond Calverley Parade, was the Opera House (page 165), opened in 1902, and to the left, the Congregational Church, essentially the same building that we tend to call 'Habitat' today, though surrounded in 1909 by a fence and thick hedge. Into Monson Road and we find two examples of civic enterprise from the days before the Ratepayers' League took over - the Technical Institute (1902) and the swimming baths (1898). Monson Colonnade dated from 1889.

Then we come to the Town Hall (see opposite), which, together with the Court, and the Police and Fire Stations, occupied the corner of Calverley Road and Calverley Street, where Argos now is. Also designed by Burton, it was originally intended as a

market. They hated it in 1909. The *Advertiser* likened it to a

mausoleum. An otherwise complimentary article in *The Drapers' Record* said it was "certainly not attractive". Judge Emden, who, once a month, presided over the County Court, threatened to hear his cases in Tonbridge if a new court-house were not built. The Council offered to install new windows to improve the ventilation, but a report from the Clerk to the Magistrates said "in our opinion no alteration of the existing Town Hall will render it a suitable place for the conduct of the business of a Court". The Council had bought Calverley Parade in 1895, with a view to building a new Town Hall there, but it was to take

The Council Chamber of the old Town Hall

another thirty years for this to materialise.

The land between Monson Road and Crescent Road, now taken up by the multi-storey car-park, was known as Harveytown, and comprised two very different types of housing. At the Monson Road end was 'Cadogan House' which, until 1905, had been the vicarage of Holy Trinity Church. It was a fine old house, with perhaps 11 bedrooms, in gardens of ¾ acre, and valued, in 1915, at £6,800. Just 30 feet away was Hervey Court - 22 tiny cottages, two-up and two-down, with yards but no gardens - accessed by two alley-ways between the houses in Crescent Road (below). Rents were typically 4/6 to 5/- a week. Joan Burslem thought them "squalid little houses"

and was frightened of passing the entrance because "wild-looking and ragged children would shout at one". In 1901 there were 39 children living there, mostly in families of two or three, though in one house there were nine. The occupiers were mainly labourers and laundresses. It is nice to find personal details of people living in groups like this, who usually appear only in official statistics; details like the will of Mary Pratley, who died in 1908, and who left "my best blanket" to her mother, Mrs Honess, at no. 13.

Calverley Road

Calverley Road in 1909 was lined with shops. Drapers and outfitters, certainly, with Waymarks at one end, and Noakes at the other (see opposite). But there were also many food shops: Carr's the grocers at Carr's Corner; a collection of multiples: International, Lipton's and Maypole, in the centre where Starbucks is now; but also many independents: butchers (three), green-grocers, dairies, bakers, and more grocers. Roberts, at no. 11 was proud of its patent bacon slicer: all rashers of equal thickness. There was also the Baptist Tabernacle, and market stalls along the sunny side - though only from 1pm to 11pm on Saturdays. It was not a shopping street that was generally patronised by the more genteel residents of the town, certainly not on a Saturday, and certainly not as the afternoon wore on, and the

drunks emerged. They were more likely to use Raiswell's the grocers on Mount Pleasant or Durrant's on the Pantiles.

The picture above shows Noakes in its original position, in Calverley House, which was designed in 1897 by HM Caley . Below, the view looking west shows the Baptist Tabernacle. It also shows: Tickner's on the extreme right of the picture - Joan Burslem remembered the powerful smell of their cheeses; and the Fountain Tavern, the small building with the gables. Golding Street is next to it.

171

Right: The Salvation Army Citadel in Varney Street. Opened in 1884, it occupied part of the site of the town's original gas works. Today (2008) it would be under the rear section of Woolworth.

Below: The Salvation Army band in Market Road (between Varney and Golding Streets) in front of the Tunbridge Wells Laundry (see page 70).

Left: Ely Lane looking towards Calverley Road.

Between the shops on Calverley Road, four narrow entrances: Basinghall Lane, Varney Street, Golding Street and Ely Lane, led into the tightly packed area that is now covered by Royal Victoria Place - cottages, tenements, workshops, smithies, slaughterhouses, two schools, a laundry and the Salvation Army**.

The area currently covered by the Royal Victoria Place shopping mall, in 1909 a tightly-packed residential and semi-industrial area.

**In 1901, 939 people lived in the total area bounded by Calveley, Camden, Victoria, Goods Station and Grosvenor Roads. 589 lived in the five inner streets: Ely Lane, Golding Street, Market Road, Varney Street and Basinghall Lane.

Calverley Park Gardens and Pembury Road

The South Ward extended eastwards to include the larger houses along Calverley Park Gardens and Pembury Road, a different world from the back streets off Camden Road. Let us take just one as an example: Shandon Court, on Pembury Road. Originally a William Willicombe house called Rosebank, it was extensively re-modelled by Sir Mervyn Macartney in the 1890's for Charles Fletcher-Ludwidge. He was mayor four times in the days when the progressives dominated the council, and was much involved with the building of the Technical Institute and the swimming baths. Fletcher-Ludwidge died

Ion Perdicaris

in 1907. The occupier in 1909 had a very different background. Ion Perdicaris was a wealthy Greek American who had lived in Tangier for many years. Morocco was something of a hot-spot during this period. It was under French influence, but not yet a French colony. Germany twice sought to test the Anglo-French 'entente' by sending warships there. In 1904 Perdicaris was taken hostage by a Moroccan bandit leader called Raisuli, who demanded a ransom of $70,000. The Sultan at first refused to react, but when the *USS Brooklyn* turned up with a detachment of Marines, and President Roosevelt declared that he wanted 'Perdicaris alive, or Raisuli dead', means were found to release him. Perdicaris came to Tunbridge Wells in 1907, and stayed until 1910.

In August, Mr Perdicaris opened the grounds of Shandon for the annual children's outing of the Tunbridge Wells Co-operative Society** in Kensington Street. Eight hundred adults and children marched in procession along Camden Road with banners and flags, led by a military band and decorated lorries. There was a programme of sports and then tea at 4:30 with lemonade for all. Each child received a handkerchief and a packet of toffee, and the opportunity to win prizes. The best prizes went to the winners of the boot-cleaning and spoon-polishing competitions.

** It had 720 members in October 1909.

The North Ward

- **Culverden**

- **St John's**

- **Woodbury Park**

- **Grosvenor Road**

Please see map on page 200.

175

Culverden

The North Ward started at the junction of Mount Ephraim and London Road - where the Common narrows to a point, and the cabs and bath-chairs waited for business. This first part of the North Ward we might call Culverden. The building on the right was Williams' Library.

The buildings have not changed much since 1909, though some of the ground floors are now shops. Further along Mount Ephraim, though, was Emmanuel Church, with its very slender spire, built in 1867. The church was part of the Countess of Huntingdon's Connexion. It had been one of the more prominent non-conformist churches in the town, but ten or so years earlier there had been a split in the congregation, and a hundred or so had left to form St John's Free Church - just across the road - see opposite. By 1909 Emmanuel had sufficiently re-established itself to organise the annual Christmas meal for the needy (see page 4).

70 *TUNBRIDGE WELLS.*
Mount Ephraim. — LL.

176

Behind the shops on the west side stood Great Culverden, a Decimus Burton house of the late 1820's, in a park of 100 acres. It was the home of Admiral Charles Davis Lucas. As a 20 year-old midshipman serving in the Crimean War he earned the first ever VC, for throwing overboard a live shell which had landed on the deck of his ship. In 1909 he was chairman of the North Ward Conservative Association. Great Culverden was demolished in 1927 - the land was used for the Kent & Sussex Hospital. Emmanuel Church was then demolished in 1974 to improve access.

At the junction of Mount Ephraim and Grosvenor Road there was a drinking fountain in the middle of the road. To have a fountain in such a position says a lot about the level of traffic in 1909. The fountain is now in the Woodbury Park Cemetery. The building behind it was St John's Free Church (now the United Reform Church), designed in 1901 by HM Caley.

177

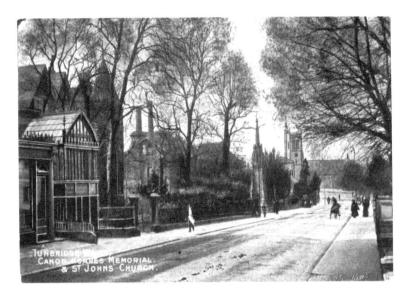

Tunbridge Canon Hoares Memorial & St Johns Church.

The shop with conservatory on the extreme left in the picture above was WC Holland's florists - which would have become the 'Royal Tunbridge Wells Horticultural Establishment" had the Home Office agreed (see page 80). The picture also shows the Hoare Memorial (1897) in its original position - in the middle of Culverden Park road; and the tower of St John's Church, which was added in 1897.

Through the trees are the chimneys of Kelsey's brewery. There had been a brewery on this site for more than 150 years, owned by Kelseys since the 1850's. In 1909 it was run by EM and AR Kelsey, sons of one of the original two Kelsey brothers. The company had over 100 pubs in Kent, Surrey and Sussex. It was taken over in 1948, and the brewery closed in 1962.

The brewery offices were in an attractive building on St Johns

178

Road. The picture (left) is from the 1960's, but the building had not changed since 1909, except that metal railings on top of the walls had been removed, and the very large gate-post on the right was new.

If you have read Richard Cobb's *Still Life*, you may remember the Limbury Buse family, living a life of 'contented ossification' in St John's. The explanation of their somnolence may be that they lived at no. 25 - next door to the brewery. The Kelsey family home was at 6 Culverden Park Road - behind the brewery. The houses at the start of Culverden Park Road were large and detached - the homes of barristers, engineers, and retired Indian civil servants. By 1909, though, EM Kelsey had gone even further up-market with a new house on Culverden Down, and so was a near neighbour of Alfred Hicks, stockbroker and ex-mayor (1906) at 'Culverden Castle', and Claude Cayley**, Vice Commodore of the Royal London Yacht Club at 'Huntleys'.

The houses along both sides of this stretch of St Johns Road had front gardens with lawns and hedges. Opposite the brewery, though, was the St Johns Sanitary Laundry - "a high-class modern laundry dealing with Best Family Washings only". The laundry had machines which soaked, washed, boiled, rinsed, blue'd and starched the clothes, but the most impressive was the 'hydro-extractor', which took "every bit of moisture out". They used special drying rooms with slightly warmed and filtered air, so that there was no chance of smuts or germs. They also took in washing from London which required 2 or 3 extra washings because of the fog and smoke there. According to the *Society* reporter, "the

** Cayley owned a racing schooner called 'Adela'. On at least two occasions he raced it against the Kaiser's 'Meteor' (and lost). It was restored in 1995.

very nicest collection of girls and women is found at St John's. The employees are only selected from the better classes of laundry workers ... They also look a very nice, healthy and happy set of women".

St John's and the Lew

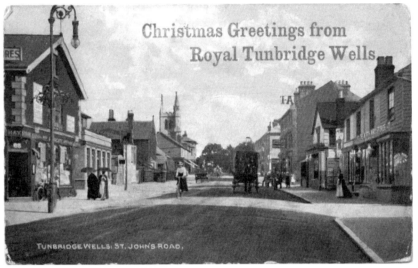

The picture above, showing St John's Road from the north, was overprinted with the town's new name in 1909 (the card was posted on Dec 22nd) but it's difficult to be sure of the date of the actual picture. On the left is Scott's coal and corn merchant, then the Red Lion, then an area which in 1909 was Invicta Motors, then an ivy-covered house and then St John's School. In another picture dated 1905, the ivy has gone from the house, so this picture may be earlier than that. In 1909 the final stretch before reaching Queens Road contained private houses with front gardens.

The area to the west of this part of St Johns Road, was known as the 'Lew'. It had been developed in the 1850's. It is always described as being a 'rough area'. Certainly some of the houses there were rather primitive. An inquiry at the Town Hall in 1911 considered the condition of 14 houses owned by Cllr Vaughan Gower in what was called Albion Square. Seven of the houses had 4 rooms, seven had 2 rooms. None of them had water - they shared 2 standpipes outside in the court. Only 5 had sinks. None of them had wc's - they shared 8 in the court. Only 4 of the houses had windows in the back wall - the rest had no through ventilation.

The enquiry arose because of complaints from concerned locals: the vicar of St John's; the local Methodist minister, Mr Harold Thorpe, mayor of Tunbridge Wells in 1905, and Dr Abbott who lived at 23 St Johns Road. The main complainant though was Miss Margaret Masterman**, who had been a District Visitor for 17 years and knew the houses well. She claimed that the houses were extremely damp, being below the level of the court, and having no damp-proof course. It should be stressed that the residents, 33 adults and 16 children, did not complain. They were paying only 3/6 and 4/6 a week, and would not have found other self-contained accommodation at that price. In fact both Miss Masterman and Dr Abbott had been threatened with violence if they continued to interfere.

In 1901 most of the residents were young families with children. The heads of household were typically labourers (7) or hawkers (4). 59 out of 70 of the residents in 1901 were born in Tunbridge Wells or in nearby villages.

The various experts called to the enquiry did not accept that the houses were unfit for habitation - they were not damp, the number of wc's was within government guidelines, the recent death-rate was low. WC Cripps explained that they met the requirements of a poor and respectable class who could not afford to pay for luxuries. He even questioned whether sinks were desirable in small cottages. The Medical Officer of Health for Kent said that he would not sanction new houses of this type, but they were habitable and better than tenements. In comparion, the rent for the cheapest houses in Silverdale Road was 6s. (A labourer might earn 4d an hour - a 60 hour week would therefore generate an income of £1, but many building jobs were irregular.) The houses in Albion Square all remained in use until 1934, nos 7 to 15 until 1940.

Albion Square lay just to the north of what, in 1909, was the Wesleyan Methodist Church (which later became a dairy and is now a martial arts centre). The church had been built as a Bible Mission Hall by a local group, led by Pastor McAuliffe, but was transferred to the Wesleyans on his death in 1908.

** This was almost certainly the sister of CFG Masterman, Liberal MP and social reformer, whose book *The Condition of England* was published in 1909. He went on to lead the government's propaganda unit during the war, and introduced the concept of the war artist. Masterman's mother lived in St John's Road - first at no. 39 (opposite the church), then, from 1911, in a new house (Iona) beyond Southfield Road. Margaret and Charles are both recorded at 39 St Johns Road in the 1901 census.

The St John's area was undergoing rapid development. The Skinners' School had opened in 1887, the St John's Recreation Ground, and the Byng Hall in 1900. The football ground used by the Rangers until June 1909 became part of the site of the new County School for Girls (TWGGS), which opened in 1911. In March 1908 there were rumours that the owner of Down Farm, Mr Combley, had been negotiating with the government over a possible military barracks - surveyors were seen in the area. Nothing came of this - Crowborough seems to have been preferred.

In October the *Advertiser* reported the opening of a new furniture store at the corner of John Street. The reporter was quite ecstatic at the huge panes of plate glass and electric lights: "though the outside gave rich promise of luxuriance within, I was not prepared for the magnificence which met the eye". It demonstrated the progressive business principles of Tunbridge Wells - why shop elsewhere? - providing every accommodation for ladies, ie a 'retiring room' on every floor.

Woodbury Park, Stephens Road, Silverdale

The major developments were to the east. The previous twenty years had seen the completion of Queens Road and Woodbury Park Road. These were mainly solid middle class houses - understandably so, as they were a development by the Conservative Land Society specifically to encourage a right-voting population. That part of Woodbury Park Road between St Johns Road and the cemetery, though, included some commercial establishments, like the Autocar garage and Fry's Mineral Water plant at no.18. Fry's had started 18 years earlier with a depot at the Brighton station, then taken over Tuddenham's of Standen Street, and opened its Woodbury Park Road plant in 1900. An article in the *Advertiser* described the purpose-built 'model factory', and marvelled at the modern equipment, the cleanliness and the range of products. As well as various soda waters, it made ginger beer, lemonade, various squashes, cherry cider and kola champagne.

There were also the new developments of Stephen's Road, Hopwood Gardens, Somerset Road and Merevale Road, and further east, of Silverdale Road. Silverdale Road was actually called Shatters Road until 1903. The insertion of these new streets into what had been countryside caused some problems. The St John's Poultry Farm was having problems with the theft of eggs, so, when Herbert Henry Christian Mayes, aged 14, was caught in the act, the farmer insisted

Eastern end of
Queens Road -
junction with
Silverdale Road
(called Shatters
Road until 1903)

that he be charged. At the court he claimed that his mother had sent him, which she denied. He then admitted that he was keeping the eggs in a cupboard and eating them before the rest of the family got up in the morning. It is not clear whether he cooked them first. His mother was fined 10s.

With all the new houses there was a need for a new church at the eastern end of the St John's parish. Money was being collected for this throughout 1909. In May the Rev DJ Stather Hunt of Holy Trinity donated an entire collection to the campaign, and requested further gifts from his congregation explaining that the population of 4,000 was almost entirely poor. The new St Luke's church was opened in 1910; replacing a temporary building in Silverdale Road.

The North Ward also included Grosvenor Road (see below and over page)

A characteristic composition by James Richards of children in Grosvenor Park - a development of the early 1890's. (Compare with the picture of Kirkdale Road in the East Ward.)

183

Grosvenor Road looking north. The General Hospital to the right - on the site currently occupied (2008) by the Post Office and Noakes.

Five Ways. Sydney Jones (drapers) 'Ye Five Ways House'. Expanded next door in Oct 1909 - I think into Swan's the tobacconist.

The East Ward

22750 Tunbridge Wells. Grosvenor Recreation Grounds.

- **Camden Road - Shops and Politics**

- **Quarry Road - Industry**

- **St James and Beulah Roads**

- **Ferndale**

Please see map on page 201.

Camden Road

If the more genteel residents didn't like to shop in Calverley Road, how much more so did that apply to Camden Road - the "populous area behind the old Town Hall" of which Richard Cobb, who grew up in Grove Hill Road, knew nothing. The East Ward started at the junction of Camden Road and Garden Road and beyond this the shops just got smaller. Joan Burslem remembered buying corsets, stockings and combinations there. Perhaps she was attracted by the 'Royal' brand at Scott's (see left), which occupied nos. 70 to 76. It boasted of serving 800 customers a week, and offered 1/- in the £ discount on tickets from clothing clubs.

It is the politics that most appeals about Camden Road. To take a phrase from *Ragged Trousered Philanthropists*: "some of them were under the delusion that they were Conservatives: similarly, others imagined themselves to be Liberals". And so it was in Camden Road. No. 141 housed the Conservative Working Men's Institute, which provided a platform for Conservative politicians campaigning on local and national issues. There may, of course, have been an element of self-interest about this, the Institute offered the services of its members as gardeners, chauffeurs and coachmen, to Conservative employers. So Camden Road was no hot-bed of radical politics, but it did have those who were struggling against the status quo.

Kirkdale Rd looking towards Camden Rd. There was a smithy behind the house on the left.

James Richards and his wife ran a library and stationers shop at 85 Camden Road. Richards was a keen Methodist preacher, and a photographer (the picture below left for example). He was also active in local politics. He was elected to the Council in 1905 as the 'working man's representative', but defeated in 1908. He insisted that he would continue the fight against the Ratepayers' League, in or out of the Council.

Julian Taylor, who lived in Albion Road, was organiser of the Social Democratic Party. They held debates and gave lectures. In 1908 they invited Paget Hedges to debate the question "Should the Working Class support the Liberal Party". Mr Hedges did not think that "any useful purpose would be served" by such a meeting.

Primitive Methodist Church
Camden Road

The Rev Mr Potter of the Primitive Methodist church in Camden Road went further. He was quoted in October as explaining that it was indisputedly the teaching of Christ to eliminate selfishness, and that it was only by the State controlling all wealth that the dream of Jesus could be reached in ordinary humanity. "If Jesus had lived in these times, he would have been a Socialist."

On 1st November Richard's 1908 defeat was avenged when HT Berwick topped the East Ward poll against two Ratepayers' candidates. Berwick lived in Upper Grosvenor Road. In 1907 he had come a poor fifth with only 159 votes. In 1909 he gained 598 - perhaps his activities for the Right to Work committee earlier in the year were being recognised. The *Courier* was not pleased: "The East Ward has the unfortunate reputation of having deprived the Council of some of it best members". But the *Courier* was also to be avenged, for a by-election was called later that the month, "an opportunity" it said "of repairing the unfortunate error of judgement". And so it happened, for this was the election that resulted in the overwhelming victory for Vaughan Gower (see page 136).

Quarry Road

St Barnabas' Church was well-establised by 1909. The parish had been split off from St James' in 1881, and the church consecrated in 1893. Like many Anglo Catholic churches it served a very poor area, but was able to draw on the support, and funds, of wealthier families from a wider area (such as the Sassoons - see page 60). St Barnabas dominated the area, but for those of a different religious persuasion there was the Christian Meeting Room in Commercial Road and a Gospel Hall in Quarry Road. These were not just for meetings and prayer: they also had weddings and funerals.

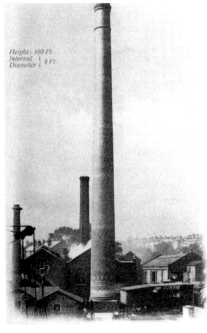

Height: 150 Ft.
Internal } 8 Ft.
Diameter }

At the bottom of Quarry Road, behind St Barnabas' School, was the town's electricity station - founded in 1895, at the peak of enthusiasm for municipal trading. During the annual inspection in November it was besieged by 150 councillors and burgesses keen to experience the "awe-inspiring" new turbine engine. Some of the councillors had a problem - they were excited about the plant, but they didn't think that the Council should own it. The Mayor, who didn't object to public ownership, said that they had a fine asset in which they had invested £100,000. Cllr Tyler, who did object, nevertheless accepted that the town benefitted from electricity at £45 per kW, when Eastbourne was paying £94. He looked forward to a time when the new filament bulbs would be cheap enough for domestic lighting - it would mean only having to decorate every fifteen years (gaslighting was notoriously dirty - one reason that spring-cleaning was so necessary every year). In June the Council announced that it was converting 200 street lamps to electricity (out of a total of c 600 I think). The *Courier* didn't approve - gas lighting was cheaper.

It is not clear whether the very tall chimney (see above) was in place in 1909, I think it might have been. It seems unlikely, though, that the three wooden cooling towers were - though they dominate later pictures of the scene. Frank Eling, who was born in 1908, attended St James' Infants and Junior schools. These were on the eastern side of Quarry Road. His memory is that the classrooms were always damp as a result of the cooling tower which was located between Albion Road and Western Road. Another long-time resident spoke of Quarry Road as the street of eternal drizzle.

In February four 'lads' were fined 1/- each for playing football on Quarry Road. Perhaps this was for their own safety; perhaps they were just being a nuisance. Certainly the road could be dangerous, a young cyclist died in June in a collision with a brewery van coming out of Stanley Road. There must have been a lot of freight traffic - from the corporation yard at the bottom of Quarry Road; from the Medway coal 'wharves' behind lower St James' Road; and from the timber yard behind the St James' Schools (see picture below). There were timber yards throughout the area: Good Station Road, Kensington Street, Beech Street, and just across Grosvenor Bridge. The picture demonstrates the reality of saw mills - that they involve handling lots of very large tree trunks; and these tree trunks, and the resulting planks, need to be transported. In December a wheel came off a timber tug hauling two tree trunks along Camden Road. It blocked the road for two hours. The cost of local transportation was high - contracts for coal to be delivered to the Pembury Water Works, for example, quoted 23/9 per ton for the coal to be dug in South Wales and transported 166 miles to the railway station in Tunbridge Wells, and then a further 3/4 a ton, for it to be carted

The timber yard behind St James' schools in Quarry Road. Picture by courtesy of Brian Woodgate. The cooling tower was later on this site.

three miles to Pembury.

The Grosvenor Bridge was opened in 1883. In 1887 one of the arches at the St James' Road end was converted into a mortuary, and in 1888 regulations were effected that in all cases of death, other than in a private house, the body was to be taken there. Arrangements were made for it to be cleaned when required (at a cost of 7/6 a quarter), and for the police to check for vandalism once a week. It was still in use in 1909, though there were complaints about inconvenience to coroner's juries, who had to view the body under Grosvenor Bridge, then return to the Town Hall for the inquest.

Between the mortuary and the Medway coal wharves was the entrance to the Grosvenor Recreation Ground (see page 185) and the open-air swimming baths. The park was opened in 1889, the work of the distinguished landscape designer Robert Marnock. It had an ornamental lake, a bandstand, and tennis courts, but Richard Cobb remembered it from the 1920's as "potentially dangerous, at least for middle-class children". Perhaps it was in 1909 too, but Richard Cobb does seem to have been an excessively sensitive child.

The streets south of the park, from Auckland and Rochdale Roads up to St James' Church, were essentially complete by the 1880's; St James' Park was built around 1900, and Dorking Road only half-built by 1909. As one moved up the hill towards the church, so the wealth and social standing of the residents increased, though not to the levels of some parts of town. At no 3 St James Road, lived Charles Prior, aged 50, the Chief Constable of the Tunbridge Wells. He had

been due to retire in 1909 but persuaded the Council that it would be cheaper to retain him at a salary of £420, rather than to give him a pension and pay for a successor.

Left: Entrance to the Medway coal wharves at the bottom of St James' Road (probably later than 1909.)
Right: Steam lorry (1909)

Just around the corner at 2 Beulah Road was 'Illawarra', the home (until at least 1906) of CM Doughty (left), traveller and author.

As a young man he had spent two years travelling in Arabia, and then ten years writing up his notes, in a poetic style supposedly based on the King James Bible. He refused all attempts by his editors to make it more 'accessible': "It is chaste and right English of the best time and without a word of costermongery". *Travels in Arabia Deserta* wasn't a success, and Doughty was forced to live abroad where life was cheaper. He met his wife, a grand-daughter of General Napier (he who had sinned) in Italy. In 1898 they returned to England, to Tunbridge Wells: "we think before all of the little ones, and their health is best in the fresh but uncomfortable English climate". They had two daughters, an Italian governess, Swiss cook, and an Italian housemaid.

Beulah Road, even at its best, was not up to the standard of the houses that he had grown up in, nor of those that they had enjoyed in Italy; but Doughty was not interested in financial success. While at Illawarra, he wrote another long poem *Dawn in Britain*, rather to the despair of his publishers. It did, however, appeal to the young Sassoon, who wrote to him, not realising that he lived so close. Doughty was a scholarly and meticulous author, but he could also produce trite, jingoistic nonsense such as *The Cliffs*, in 1909 - Doughty was one of those who feared an invasion. Doughty's reputation, and that of *Arabia Deserta* was just beginning to emerge in 1909. It was later to be consolidated by the enthusiastic support of TE Lawrence.

St James' was the biggest parish in Tunbridge Wells and probably one of the busiest, with ten services each Sunday. The vicar, the Ven AT

Scott was also *ex-officio* chaplain of the workhouse. Archdeacon Scott lived behind the church in Ferndale, a rather more select area. The pattern of the houses shown on the map below, with their big gardens, contrasts sharply with St James' Road and St James' Park. The biggest, in the centre, was 'The Dell', four storeys, 13 bedrooms, a lake, tennis courts, vinery and two peach houses, nine acres in all. It was valued at £8,000 though was considered "somewhat old-fashioned". To the east was 'Larchwood' , six acres, 9 bedrooms and a boudoir, and a garden "a la Versailles". On the opposite side, nos.

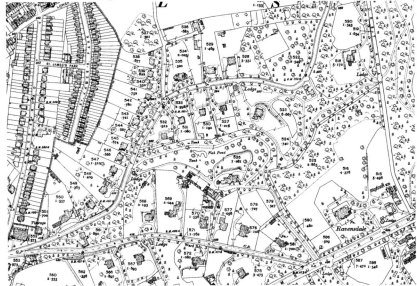

31 (Humboldt House) and 33 were of similar value. John Smith Weare, founder of the High Brooms Brickworks had lived in the area - his son still owned some of the houses.

Archdeacon Scott was something of a sportsman. Born on the same day as WG Grace, it was fitting that he should play cricket for Cambridge. He also did the pole jump. In 1888 he was one of the founders of the Ashdown Forest and Tunbridge Wells Golf Club, hitting the first stroke on Christmas Eve that year. In June 1893 the club applied to the Home Office for the right to use the prefix 'Royal', but perhaps you are getting a sense of déjà vu here. In this case the petition had the support of the Duke of Cambridge. The memo to the Queen simply suggested: "Your Majesty will probably allow this Golf Club the title of Royal". Things are so much easier when you have the right connections.

Conclusion

My intention in putting together this book was only to describe, not to comment on, or to criticise, or to draw conclusions. I wrote it simply because I wanted to understand what it was like to live in 1909. Of course any selection is subjective, and my own interests and prejudices must be obvious. You would not imagine, for example, from reading these pages, that gardening was a popular hobby in 1909, that more column inches were dedicated to horticultural societies than to Cricket Week and the Agricultural Show put together. I have dwelt especially on aspects of life of which I hadn't previously been aware - like the motor-cycle racing at the Nevill, but I did not deliberately avoid other aspects. Yet the Tunbridge Wells that I discovered was not the town that I might have expected, not the "wonderfully secure and lavish world of Edwardian England" in Richard Cobb's words. Certainly the residents were class-ridden, ageist, sexist, racist, sectarian and probably homophobic, and labelled any change that they didn't like as 'faddish'. But there were some, and one warms to them, who embraced the new: motor cars, aeroplanes, telephones and electric lights, certainly; but also postcards and thermos flasks; and 'rinking', and jig-saw puzzles and votes for women.

I rather hoped that the local papers would have taken the occasion of New Year 1910 to present a review of 1909, but both *Courier* and *Advertiser* were too focused on the election to think about looking back. The *Advertiser* was especially excited. It reminded readers that only 12 Conservative MP's had voted for Old Age Pensions, and came up with the hope that "The nation will now ... destroy once and for all time the arrogant pretensions of the unrepresentative Peers". It did however have time to praise the work of the Advertising Association, and mentioned in passing that they had worked with the Mayor to get the 'Royal' prefix for the town. The *Gazette* did have a formal review of the year. It also praised the Advertising Association, but didn't mention the prefix.

I looked for statistics by which we might measure the success of the various advertising activities. All I found was a report from the LB&SCR that passenger numbers to Tunbridge Wells showed no increase over the year. Disappointing, but then the LB&SCR was only one route into the town. I tried a search of the *Times* - to see how much the 'Royal' prefix was being used over the following years.

It appeared mainly in estate agents' advertisements. There was one interesting use though, from November 1914, and again it was from an advert:

"Royal Tunbridge Wells, the sunny Kentish Health Resort, has many claims for consideration at the present time, for, besides being the Nearest Inland Resort to London, its restful and peaceful atmosphere is practically unaffected by the turmoil of the war."

There, on the the last page, I have broken my resolution not to mention that word - that event which so dominates most histories and memoirs of the late Edwardian period. I tried, rather, to present 1909 through the eyes of those who were living at the time - knowing only what they knew; though being aware of what was about to happen did add a certain sombreness to the exercise.

I would love to be able to explain what happened afterwards to the skating rink, and the workhouse, Siegfried Sassoon, the unemployed, Clara Bassett, the boys who were birched, and the rest of them, but the task is just too big. I must, though, tidy up a couple of loose ends. The general election took place on January 20th 1910. Nationally, the Conservatives gained over a hundred seats but were still beaten by a Liberal-led coalition. In Tunbridge the Conservative victory was emphatic. Spender Clay won a majority of 3,210. On May 6th the King died. He had been ill for some time, but his death came suddenly and surprised the nation. Political manoevring was suspended for a few weeks.

King Edward the man was no more, but the King Edward potato, advertised for the first time in 1910, has been a best-seller ever since. Now that really is an example of successful 'royal' branding.

Appendices

Appendix A - Population Statistics

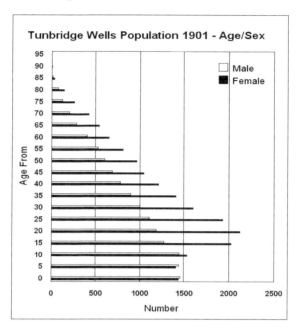

1909 falls between the two census years of 1901 and 1911. The government produced a wealth of statistics from the 1911 figures, but unfortunately Tunbridge Wells was not quite big enough to be separately represented in them. The most striking thing about the population in 1901 was the difference in numbers between males and females over the age of 15 - a ratio of 1:1.65. A large part of this difference - c 3,400 out of just over 6,000 - is attributable to the number of female servants, but clearly that it not the whole story. If we assume that most of the servants were in the younger age-bands, then the male-female split amongst the older population becomes all the more striking.

Appendix B - The Royal Connection

A Home Office minute of February 1909 says that Leamington Spa was allowed 'Royal' in 1838, but "that was before these privileges were carefully looked into". So what was it about the Tunbridge Wells claim, that stood up to a more rigorous scrutiny?

The Mayor opened his petition with references to Henrietta Maria and Catherine of Braganza, 17th century wives of Charles I and Charles II. Henrietta Maria came in 1629 to recuperate after the death of a premature child. At the time there were no significant buildings nearby, so the royal party stayed in tents on Bishop's Down. Catherine of Braganza visited at least three times in the 1660's, on one occasion at Christmas. She tended to stay for some weeks, with the King coming down to join her whenever business allowed. Some stories say that they stayed in Mount Ephraim House, others that it was at Great Bounds in Southborough.

The later Stuarts, James II and his family, were also visitors. Princess, later Queen, Anne, visited for season after season, and is said to have contributed £100 for the paving of the Walks. These were not mentioned by the mayor, and he rather skipped over the Hanoverians too, claiming only that they were "constant visitors" in the 18th century.

The best known, and most loved of the royal visitors, was the young Princess Victoria, who came with her mother, the Duchess of Kent, on four occasions in the 1820's and 1830's. They stayed, variously, at Mount Pleasant House (now the Hotel du Vin) and at Boyne House on Mount Ephraim. During her visits she attended services at Holy Trinity and King Charles the Martyr; went to the races on the Common; and performed various ceremonial functions, such as opening the Royal Victoria School. On some of the visits they were accompanied by Victoria's half-sister, the Princess Feodore. The Mayor also mentioned the Princess Louise, Victoria's daughter, who lived for a while at Dornden in Rusthall, during the 1870's.

Clearly the civil servants were not impressed by the town's claim, but they seem to have left the decision to the King. He had turned down the request over the Opera House. Perhaps this time he remembered his mother reminiscing about her holidays here as a child. Lady Dorothy Nevill once found some dried flowers that had been presented to Eridge by the young princess. They were described as the only flowers that her garden in Tunbridge Wells ever produced. That has a rather forlorn ring to it, but that isn't how Victoria herself remembered her visits. In 1835, at the end of her last visit she wrote in her diary: "I am very sorry to leave the dear place. I am so very fond of it." And it was very fond of her. Seventy four years later it got its reward.

Sources

Newspapers and Periodicals:

Kent & Sussex Courier (Tunbridge Wells Ref Library)
Tonbridge Free Press (Tonbridge Ref Library)
Tunbridge Wells Society (British Library, Colindale)
Tunbridge Wells Advertiser (BL Colindale)
The Tunbridge Wells Gazette and Fashionable Visitors List (BLColindale)
The Times (on-line archive via KCC Libraries)
Illustrated London News (Worcester Ref Library, but available generally)
Annual Register (Worcester Ref Library, but available generally)
Punch (private collection but available generally)

Archives:

Amelia Scott papers (Women's Library at London Metropolitan University)
Tonbridge Union (workhouse) papers (Centre for Kentish Studies Maidstone)
Minutes of Tunbridge Wells Borough Council (TW Council Archives)
Minutes of Tonbridge Rural District Council (TW Council Archives)
Valuation Office papers** (The National Archives, Kew)
Home Office papers (TNA Kew)

Miscellaneous:

Pelton's and Kelly's directories and guide books (TW Ref Library)
Bracketts Sales Catalogues (TW Ref Library)
1901 Census. (TW Ref Library, and on CD)
1901/1911 Census. Summary tables on *histpop.org* (website)
Ordnance Survey maps 1909 edition 1:2500 (TW Ref Library)
A Peep into the Past Clements, RHM (1939?) (TW Ref Library)
Where Old and New Meet Townsend, Rev JH (1910?) (TW Ref Library)
TWGirls Grammar Sschool 1905 - 1980 (TW Ref Library)
TWHigh School Jubilee Record 1883 - 1933 (TW Ref Library)
Second Triennial Report on Higher Education in Kent KEC (1910) (Ton Ref Library)
Kent at the opening of the 20th Century / Contemporary Biographies Bavington Jones and Pike (1904) (in private collection)
The Internet provides access to a wide range of information, eg: the archives of *The New York Times,* the DNB, burial records for TWBC cemetery on *deceasedonline.com,* and the excellent *workhouse.org*

Unpublished:

Memories of Joan Burslem (typescript, available from TW Ref Library)
Memories of Frank Eling (typescript in private collection)
The Admission of the Elderly into the Tonbridge Union Workhouse 1880-1930 Vera Coomber (MSc dissertation KCL 1996)
Minutes of the Cricket Week Amusement Committee (private collection)
Material collected by Richard Gosling and Graham Edwards for a history of the Scouts (private collection)

Architect's plans for the Tunbridge Wells Club (Burns Guthrie partners)

Published:

Arnim, Elizabeth von The Caravanners (1909)

Bassett, Roger W *Better Then Than Now* (2008)

Bech, D & Mahler, K *Historical and Interesting Views of T. Wells* (2004) (CD)

Bennett, Arnold *Old Wives' Tale* (1908)

Boorman & Maskell *Tonbridge Free Press Centenary* (1969)

Boscawen, AST *Fourteen Years in Parliament* (1907)

Chadwick, Owen *The Victorian Church* (1970)

Cobb, Richard *Still Life Sketches from a Tunbridge Wells Childhood* (1984)

Cunningham, J (ed) *The Residential Parks of Tunbridge Wells* (2004), (ed) *400 Years of the Wells* (2005), *The Origins of Warwick Park and the Nevill Ground* (2007), (ed) *An Historical Atlas of Tunbridge Wells* (2007)

Baldock, Eric *Transport in Kent - A Selection of Old Postcards* (1991)

Buettner, Elizabeth *Empire Families: Britain and Late Imperial India* (2004)

Butcher, Josephine *Tunbridge Wells I was born on the Pantiles* (1990)

Daily News, The *The Wonderful Year 1909* (1910?)

Ensor, RCK *England 1870-1914* (1936)

Farrance, Sheila & Bennett, Jacqueline *Memoirs of a Village Rectory* (1993)

Foreman, Don *Royal Visitors to Tunbridge Wells* (1993)

Forster, EM *A Room with a View* (1908)

Fowler, Simon *Workhouse The People The Places The Life ...* (2007)

Grahame, Kenneth *The Golden Age* (1895) , *Dream Days* (1898), *The Wind in the Willows* (1908)

Grand, Sarah *Emotional Moments* (1908)

Green,Peter *Beyond the Wild Wood -The World of Kenneth Grahame* (1982)

Harrison, Shirley *Sylvia Pankhurst A Crusading Life* (2003)

Hatcher, Dorothy *The Workhouse and the Weald* (1988)

Hattersley, Roy *The Edwardians* (2004)

Hetherington & Griffiths *Old Pubs of Tunbridge Wells & District* (1986)

Higgs, Michelle *Life in the Victorian and Edwardian Workhouse* (2007)

Hope, Lady *English Homes and Villages (Kent and Sussex)* (1909)

Horn, Pamela *Life Below Stairs in the 20th Century* (2001)

King, John *Buses and Bathchairs, but not a Tram in Sight* (1976)

McLeod, Kirsty *The Last Summer May to September 1913* (1983)

Marchant, Edward *One Cog* (St Augustine's Church) (?1992)

Masterman, CFG *The Condition of England* (1909)

Melville, Lewis *Society at Tunbridge Wells ...* (1912)

Nevill, Lady Dorothy *Under Five Reigns* (1910), *My Own Times* (1912)

Nevill, Guy *Exotic Groves a Portrait of Lady Dorothy Nevill* (1984)

Nicholson, Juliet *The Perfect Summer Dancing into Shadow in1911* (2006)

Pearsall, Ronald *Edwardian Life and Leisure* (1973)

Ponsonby, Sir Frederick *Recollestions ofThree Reigns* (1951)

Pugh, Martin *The Pankhursts* (2001)

Punch *Mr Punch's Cavalcade (1900 - 1930) A Review of Thirty Years* (c1933)

Roberts, John Stuart *Siegfried Sassoon* (1999)

Rowlands & Beavis *Tunbridge Wells in Old Photgraphs* (2 vol) (1991, 1994)
Rowley, Christopher *We had Everything ... Leigh 1900-2000* (2000)
Sassoon, Siegfried *Memoirs of a Fox-Hunting Man* (1928), *The Old Century and Seven More Years* (1938), *The Weald of Youth* (1942)
Taylor, Andrew *God's Fugitive - The Life ofCharles Montagu Doughty* (1999)
Tressell, Robert *The Ragged Trousered Philanthropists* (1914)
Wells, HG *The History of Mr Polly* (1910), *Tono-Bungay* (1909)
Winter, Gordon *The Golden Years (1902-1913)* (1975)

** The Valuation Office papers are an extremely important resource for local historians, and were the direct result of the 1909 Budget. To be able to tax any increase in the value of land, as Lloyd George had proposed, one needed an initial valuation from which the increase could be measured. The Valuation Office was set up to do this, and by 1915 had completed valuations for properties across most of England and Wales. The valuations for Ferndale, for example, were done in July 1912. The valuations give a detailed description of eachproperty: owner, occupier, number of rooms, type of construction, and actual or estimated rent. They can include interesting detail. Wadham Elers' house in Bishop's Down, for example, which was owned by the Lord of the Manor, was described as 'not in good repair'

Maps

On the following four pages are extracts of the 1909 Ordnance Survey maps showing the central part of Tunbridge Wells. The four maps correspond very broadly to the four wards, and are in the sequence: North, East, West and South.

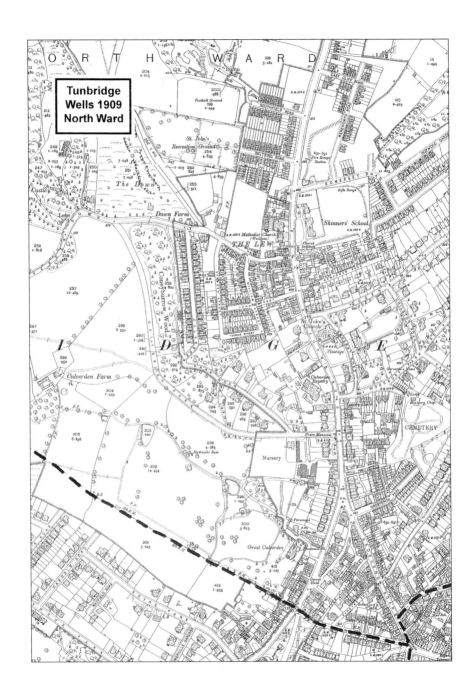

Tunbridge
Wells 1909
North Ward

200

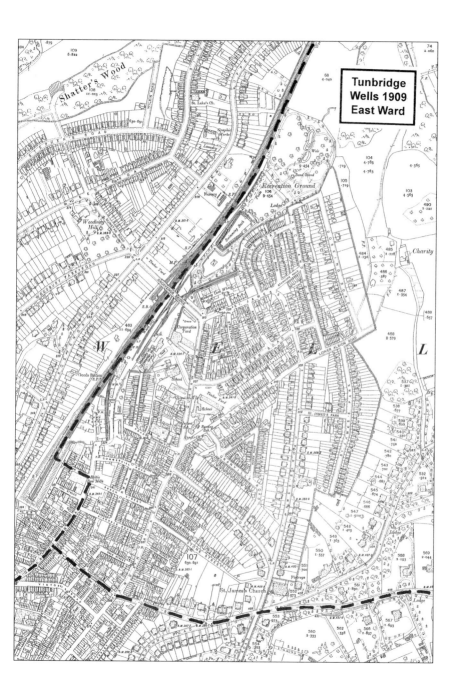

Tunbridge
Wells 1909
East Ward

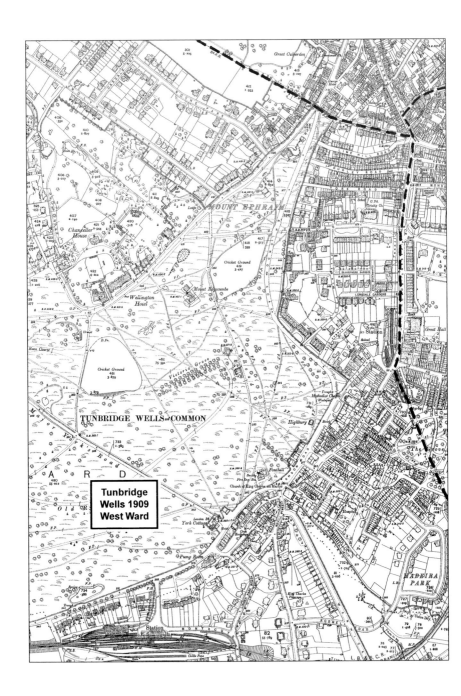

Tunbridge
Wells 1909
West Ward

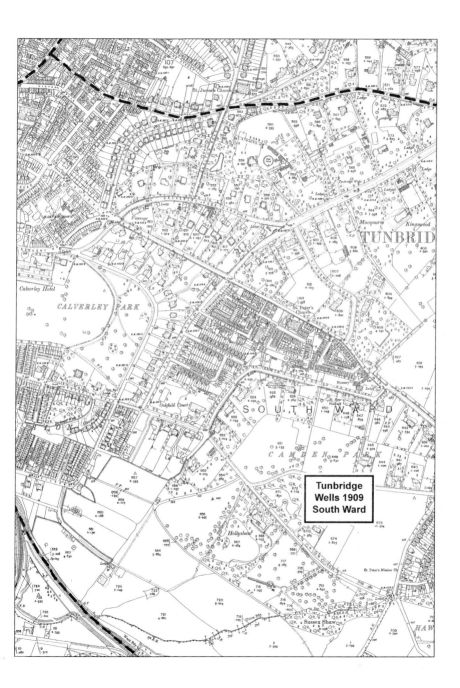

Tunbridge
Wells 1909
South Ward

Index